Women and Community Action

Lena Dominelli

Publisher Jo Campling

Venture Press

Venture Press Limited
16 Kent Street
Birmingham
B5 6RD

First published 1990

To all women struggling to be free

Design and production by Saxon Publishing Consultants
Limited
Typeset in 10/11 Baskerville by TecSet Limited
Printed and bound by Hartnolls Limited, Bodmin, Cornwall

ISBN 0 90010 2 772

Acknowledgements

The 'community' is popularly acknowledged as women's place. Yet, work women undertake in the community, on behalf of the community is largely invisible, making women seem part of the community, whilst being excluded from it. Community action has drawn on women's struggles to gain a real voice in their communities and foster social change at the local level. The heroic efforts of women who have fought to reshape their world in more humane directions underpin this book. Though without names to highlight their contribution, I am grateful to them.

My heartfelt thanks also go out to all those who have enabled me to free my mind and time for writing this book. These include my mother, my father, my sister Maria, and my brother Nic who looked after my baby son, Nicholas; Rita Thodes, for her typing, and her husband Matt for sacrificing his evenings with her; my husband David for his loving understanding and support; and Nicholas, who despite babyhood, grasped the meaning of 'Mama Work' and played with 'Nonna' (my mother). Finally, many thanks to Gudrun Jonsdottir and Kwenna Frambothid for their encouragement and permission to draw on materials from COMMUNITY ACTION (1982).

l.d.

Contents

Introduction
Women and Community Work

Community work exists in a variety of forms. These range from traditional approaches, drawing on informal community networks and resources present in communities, to the more challenging forms of community organisation developed by working class activists, feminists and black people. Definitions of community work activities have referred to 'hard' issues related to the economic infrastructure (for example, employment and housing) and 'soft' issues associated with servicing the growth of individuals or work performed by women in the community (usually in unpaid capacities, for example, playschemes and nursery places – Blagg and Derricourt, 1982). Community workers have used methods based on negotiating skills, a knowledge of community resources and direct action. The status of community work in the social work arena has been the subject of controversy for some time. Positions on this have varied from those who maintain that community work is a distinct discipline with its own traditions and political philosophy to those who consider it one method amongst many of social work intervention. (Jones and Mayo, 1974). Because both community work and social work purport to promote people's welfare, I take the view that community work is a distinct discipline which has a significant contribution to make to social work practice through its philosophy and practice. However, community work and social work use different approaches in tackling this objective.

Community work since the late 1960s has constituted a political activity through which ordinary people assert control over their communities and lives. Community work's commitment to improving the quality of life for all has been taken for granted. Despite being concerned with issues revolving around everyday life activities such as housing, the retention of community boundaries threatened by the processes of industrialisation and the provision of services to various community groups, community work has tended to ignore women's specific needs as women, whether in their own right or as carers or workers (see for example, Baldock, 1977; Vass, 1979; Winwood, 1977; Griffiths, 1974, 1979; Dale and Derricourt, 1990; Dixon, 1990). Community work has also played down the contribution women make to the community and their involvement in community action (Remfrey, 1979). Yet, women have played a major role in sustaining community action through their domestic labour, their organising skills, their commitment to community values, and their capacity to innovate (Mayo, 1977). Feminist definitions of community work have transcended traditional ones by drawing attention to women's needs for a form of community work which meets their specific needs as women, acknowledges women's contribution to their communities and community action, and demands the elimination of gender oppression. Their vehicle for achieving this has been feminist community action which provides the primary focus for this book.

Defining Community

Traditional definitions of community have focused on geographical locations and spatial arrangements based on class and kinship ties, ignoring in the process the subordinate position these have ascribed to women. A 'community' is an elusive entity, difficult to define. The process of developing a global definition reveals that there are a variety of communities and more differences between people in one 'community' than common bonds between them. The definition can encompass political, sociological, economic, geographical or religious terrains. For socialists like Ruskin, Morris and the Guild Socialists, a 'community' was an idealised concept nostalgically drawing on allegedly close supportive networks people had developed in medieval life with its rural rhythms untrammeled by machines and bound to nature (Williams, 1961). The decline of 'working class communities' has been lamented by authors like Wilmot and Young (1960) who considered planners' disregard for kinship relationships the key to the alienation featuring so strongly in modern city life. A list of definitions can be endless. Bell and Newby (1971) uncovered ninety-eight different ones about two decades ago. Since then, more have been developed. Although focusing on different aspects of 'community', these all agree that a community is a local space which is small enough for people to interact with each other. These definitions have a further common characteristic. Until feminists redressed the balance, they ignored gender (Mayo, 1977). This is strange, for women have always been present and active in the community. But even progressive activists and Marxist writers, with their emphasis on organised working class activity in the workplace, have ignored the community as a significant arena of struggle (Blagg and Derricourt, 1982). Giving primacy to social production, Marxists have relegated the community to secondary status as the site of reproduction, the place where things that did not matter in the panorama of history happened. The orthodox Marxist view of social development consigned women to a subordinate role in the unfolding of social change and reinforced the invisibility of their contribution to it. Yet, the community was the

2

place in which women lived and worked, whether or not they were involved in waged production (Wilson, 1977b). It was also where women defended the rights of their families and themselves to enjoy decent standards of living, acquire facilities enhancing their lives, and be treated with dignity and respect.

Feminist writers have tackled the neglect of gender in the theory and practice of traditional community work and made women's place in the community central to their analysis and practice. As Wilson (1977b) expresses it:

> 'The reality of community life . . . is women living in a direct relationship to the state as mediated through housing departments, schools and the State welfare system which supports the family. The division of labour within the family usually means that it is women who go to the rent office, women who attempt to grapple with the schools, women who are interviewed by the social worker.'

Women's life in the community is immersed in social relationships aimed at meeting the needs of others and mediating with state agencies on their behalf. Family life is central to these activities, so it is not surprising that women who undertake community action organise around issues such as day care facilities, housing, school closures, road widening schemes, rights to incomes and rights to jobs, which facilitate fulfilling their obligations as grandmothers, mothers, wives and daughters.

Some community workers have recognised women's role in community struggles, but in ways which have reinforced a sexist division of labour. Women without a feminist perspective have organised women's activities in ways which have reinforced women's traditional roles and domestic tasks. 'Mum's groups' are indicative of this approach. Though helpful in easing the burdens that come with childcare undertaken in the isolation of the home, giving women the opportunity to socialise with other women, and teaching women domestic skills in keeping with societal expectations of the performance of this role, these groups have not sought to transform social relations (see Davis, 1977). The lack of interest in changing society identifies such an approach as a woman-centered one rather than a feminist one. Feminists, while being woman-centered are also interested in changing society. Their community work reflects their attempts to eliminate oppressive social relations through feminist social action (Marchant and Wearing, 1986; Wilson and Weir, 1986). Male community workers have reinforced the *status quo* in other ways. They have stood by whilst men have collared prestigious community work roles and relegated women to servicing their needs in the back-rooms – making tea, typing minutes, handling routine correspondence. Or, they have acknowledged a place for women in organisational matters, but consigned them to 'soft' issues which were,

3

by definition, areas of 'women's work' and strategically less important. Women, by devoting their energies to these issues, have enabled male community workers to concentrate on the 'important', 'hard' issues emanating from economic decline in industrial communities and seek links with the trade union movement.

Feminist community workers have questioned the validity of this division and argued that struggles in the community are as important as those occurring in, or linked to, the workplace. They have also highlighted the centrality of women's roles in such struggles, recovering much of working class and black women's activist history in the process, and have also demonstrated the interdependence between workplace struggles and community struggles (Hooks, 1984; Davis, 1989). Additionally, feminists have added new dimensions to community work activity. Foremost amongst these has been the development of new ways of relating to women in collective struggles; for example, consciousness-raising; egalitarian group processes; networking; and opening up new areas of struggle (e.g., health issues, men's violence against women). They have also highlighted the importance of having a commonality of interests amongst those struggling in the community (Wilson and Weir, 1986: 41).

Community workers have traditionally defined the 'community' as the location in which they will work using one or more of the community work models at hand. Their locality based approach is often unable to surmount the contradictions and weaknesses inherent in community work. Crucial amongst these have been the lack of independent funding, inadequate facilities for supporters and competition between groups whose objectives can only be achieved at the expense of each other.

These divisions occur because community work has failed to penetrate the corridors of power in a way that will give priority to community issues and release funds for community organisation. Consequently, community groups are confined to redistributing resources amongst themselves, as in the recycling of money within the Rate Support Grant to fund the British Community Development Projects. Community workers involved in community action have attempted to overcome these deficiencies by organising their local groups in city-wide and national federations, and developing links between community action and broader mass oriented organisations such as trade unions, left political parties, and 'new social movements' (Curno, 1978). They have also developed a set of shared experiences within the groups which serve to unite them in struggle.

This book focuses on the theory and practice of feminist community action. We will consider its place in the broader context of community work, identify the processes through which it achieves its objective of fostering women's welfare in the

4

community setting and argue that feminist community work can make a useful contribution to extending the repertoire of skills held by welfare practitioners and transform their practice. The book also aims to demonstrate that the quality of life for children and men has also been enhanced through action undertaken by women on behalf of women. The book concentrates on assessing and analysing feminist community action developed since the 1960s, highlighting its accomplishments AND its limitations. By presenting some of feminist community work's main achievements, analysing the processes through which these have been reached, and identifying lessons which can be derived from it, this book will provide specific guidelines on how traditional social work and community work practice can become more involved in promoting gender equality. This book also addresses the question of overcoming divisions amongst women, particularly those based on gender, 'race' and class, and the contribution feminists sharing these concerns have made to community work theory and practice.

Chapter 1 examines traditional community work and its neglect of gender as an arena of feminist challenge. Feminist campaigns and networks form the basis of Chapter 2. Work with women on the individual level is an area of feminist activity explored in Chapter 3. The links between unpaid work in the home and waged work in the workplace have also featured strongly in feminist action. Feminist activities in the workplace are considered in Chapter 4. Chapter 5 focuses on feminist intervention in the local and central state and reveals how feminist work in these arenas is essential in underwriting the long term future of feminist community initiatives. The book concludes by highlighting feminist principles and techniques which can be used to transform traditional community work (Chapter 6). The introduction highlights models of community work and locates feminist community work within community work more generally.

Models of Community Work

Community work has a long history. It can be postulated that it began in the days when human beings first started interacting socially and recognised the potential for maximising their power by working collaboratively with those who shared their interests. However, community work was not formally recognised by western states until imperialism reached its heyday. The community work practised at that point was known as community development and was primarily concerned with industrialising non-capitalist areas of the globe and bringing them under capitalist hegemony (Marsden and Oakley, 1982; Mayo, 1975). Community work in Third World countries served to integrate colonial territories with the capitalist system by laying the foundations of a capitalist economic infrastructure, and a capitalist political superstructure within them. The

5

foundations included industrialisation, transportation, communication, education, the judiciary, state administration and Western religion (Kwo, 1984). The community development strategy incorporated the traditional ruling class in the colonial regime by according it privileged status in the civil service and local state bureaucracy in return for its support of colonial policies (Dominelli, 1974; Halpern, 1963). Through such involvement, the indigenous elite facilitated the exploitation of the indigenous masses by collecting taxes, and implementing the foreign laws legitimating private property ownership and the consequent expropriation and sale of communal lands. Following the dismantling of colonialism after World War II, community development assumed a much more overtly political role – that of preventing the spread of communism in the ex-colonies (Mayo, 1975; Marsden and Oakley, 1982).

The lessons learnt in the Third world were subsequently utilised in the expansion of state sponsored community work in the imperialist countries themselves. In Britain and the United States, the original community development models were adapted to the conditions prevailing in industrialised countries, but were primarily used to deal with working-class poverty (see Mayo, 1975). For instance, in Victorian Britain the techniques of population control, including the incorporation of local leaders and the utilisation of local resources through 'self-help' schemes, were adapted for use in the philanthropic 'Model Dwellings' constructed to relieve 'working class housing problems'. However, the American War on Poverty undertaken in the early 1960s and the British Community Development Projects begun in the late 1960s are well-known examples of recent state intervention in community work. Community workers employed under these initiatives actively involved community residents. They then discovered the fallacies of pathologising communities inherent in the community work models guiding the state's original plan of action and exposed the structural bases of inequality (Community Development Project Working Group, 1977; Braeger and Purcell, 1967). Their revelations led to the assumption of more radical community intervention known as 'community action', to counter the power of the state and capital in determining living conditions in working class communities. Though these attempts have been limited in their overall impact on existing social organisation, the state, in both Britain and America, became sufficiently concerned about its militant potential to terminate its support for radical community action. The British state is currently refining community development techniques and implementing them in Northern Ireland in its attempt to control working-class militancy there (Lovett and Percival, 1978; Griffiths, 1974).

Identifying models of community work is as problematic as defining 'the community'. The bases on which models are defined depend on features which theorists choose to delineate and are in many respects arbitrary. I am going to consider four main models of community work – community care, community development, community organisation, and community action. This division was originally developed by Rothman (1970), but I have modified it by extending the community action model and adding feminist community action and community action from a black perspective to it. There is some degree of overlap amongst the different models of community work, particularly in the areas of techniques and skills adopted. But only community action begins to examine critically the nature of capitalist social relations which underpin poverty in the modern world. The main models considered are:

* community care;
* community organisation;
* community development;
* class based community action;
* feminist community action; and
* community action from a black perspective.

Much of the literature on community work presents the community as a 'passive' entity awaiting intervention from an 'outsider' before a programme of action is set in motion (see Alinsky, 1971). The community worker is portrayed as a 'neutral' apolitical individual, interested only in implementing the 'will of the people' or 'meeting their needs' (see the 'neutral' approach reflected in the Gulbenkian Reports (1968 and 1973); Henderson *et al.* (1980); and Kramer and Specht, (1969). This picture obscures some real political realities. The first of these is the deeply political nature of this approach which endorses the *status quo*. Also hidden in its recesses is another political fact: communities are not simply passive. People in the community react to changes in their environment, adpating to the forces that come into their lives and changing these at the same time as being changed by them. Additionally the 'neutral' view of community work ignores the direction in which community work develops in response to political and economic pressures beyond the immediate control of the locality. By examining society's unequal distribution of power and resources in a fairly superficial way, for example, ignoring the gendered and racially structured nature of this distribution, neutral approaches to community work suggest that increasing 'participation' in the decision-making bodies can put matters right. This view is inadequate in societies predicated on the scarcity of resources. Redistribution can only occur at the expense of other groups which have not organised to compete with other pressure groups vying for the fulfillment of their interests.

The literature following this approach presupposes that community work is a form of pressure group politics. It assumes that the 'system' is basically sound, having merely a few wrinkles

7

which need smoothing out. Some of these wrinkles are indelible because individuals and communities are considered inadequate or pathological. As Biddle and Biddle (1965) comment: 'the poor and the alienated must overcome their inner handicap practically through the cultivation of their own initiatives.' The class, 'race' and gender biases of society remain hidden and with it, the fact that poverty, inequality, and unequally distributed power and resources are integral and necessary parts of the system. With the accumulation of wealth and power at one end of the social spectrum, misery and powerlessness are amassed at the other (Marx, 1965), creating a spiral in which the continual 'rediscovery of poverty' in the midst of affluence assumes many guises. Operating under 'neutral' approaches to the task, community work performs the vital ideological function of obscuring crucial social divisions inherent in Western society, for example, class, 'race', gender and age. In pursuing this neutral perspective, community work programmes do not actively seek to eradicate the root causes of oppression. Their main preoccupation has been to contain popular disaffection. Or, as Marris and Rein (1974) express it: 'far from challenging established power, community action turned out to be merely another instrument of social services, essentially patronising and conservative.'

The inadequate attention given to social divisions other than class in the community work literature has meant that forms of oppression other than classism have been ignored and many of the initiatives undertaken by women and black people have been discounted as community work. Traditional community work texts, e.g., *The Making of Community Work* by David Thomas, *Community Work* by Allan Twelvetrees, *Reveille for Radicals* (1969) by Saul Alinsky, virtually ignore the implications of gender and 'race'. Authors who have attempted to provide a more radical view of community work have had their analyses flawed by being both gender and colourblind, e.g., Martin Loney's *Community Against Goverment* (1983) and Paul Curno's *Political Issues in Community Work* (1978). Some texts have attempted to include gender in their analyses but have done so in a way which marginalises the feminist contribution as a chapter in a book whilst the remainder of it remains impervious to its impact, for example, *Community Work and the State* (1982) edited by Craig *et al*. The main texts which have focused primarily on women's contribution to the subject and followed feminist insights have been written by women, for example Marjorie Mayo's classic, *Women in the Community* (1977) and *Women in Collective Action* (1982) edited by Ann Curno *et al*. White authors' handling of black peoples' contribution to community work remains poor, although *Women in Collective Action* has attempted to cover 'race' and racism in some articles in the collection. However, the main text examining this issue is *Community Work and Racism* (1982) written by two black men,

8

Ashok Ohri and Basil Manning. However, these authors leave black women's community action and gender issues underexplored.

Community Care

Community work based on the community care model focuses on those social networks and voluntary services offering a direct caring service to residents, particularly sick, disabled and older persons. Women are central to this model, for they perform the bulk of the work that constitutes 'community care' (Finch, 1982; Finch and Groves, 1984). The 'Good Neighbour Scheme', 'Meals-on-Wheels', and tenants associations concerned primarily with passing information on to landlords of the improvements tenants require, exemplify this type of community work. Community workers in these schemes are usually unpaid volunteers. Women's labour often covers gaps in statutory provisions and stretches welfare state resources by providing free labour. Though the services are very much appreciated by recipients, they also feel powerless in influencing the development of provisions on offer. Powerlessness contributes to their experiencing the relationship between users and volunteers as patronising and inadequate. Service inadequacy can be partially attributed to the lack of resources. An example of this is 'Meals-on-Wheels' food reaching customers tepid or cold, because the organisation cannot spare the cash to buy equipment to keep the food warm for several hours or, conversely, food being overcooked because it is sitting in some kind of slow oven for long periods. Other serious limitations arise from the model's apolitical stance and failure to address social divisions. Thus the assumption that all individuals are the same leads to a colourblind approach which means that black people with specific religious dietary needs have these ignored (Dominelli, 1988).

Volunteers are often motivated by altruism and wanting something useful to do during their spare time. They usually consider themselves 'apolitical' and believe this political stance is reflected in the services they provide. They accept the basic soundness of the existing social system, whilst recognising that it produces problems. Ironing these out is what community care is about. The reliance of formal community care systems on volunteers means that primarily white, middle-class women, not engaged in waged work and with lighter domestic responsibilities, are free to perform these duties. Recruiting volunteers on this basis carries the danger of imposing racist, sexist and classist views of the world on those they serve, though these would be expressed as benevolent paternalism. Women, particularly white working-class and black women who cannot afford to buy the labour of other women or are refused support from the personal social services, have to undertake informal community care at home on top of their waged work and normal domestic responsibilities, or give up paid jobs when faced with additional caring demands from, for example, frail aged parents or severely disabled adult offspring (Bryan *et al*, 1985).

Community care models of community work have been promoted by the British state as part of a package of de-institutionalising care, particularly for older people. The Left's critique of institutional care has highlighted its dehumanising treatment of residents, the powerlessness imposed upon them and their neglect in places ostensibly geared to improving their welfare (Scull, 1977). These criticisms provide the foundations on which governments, pressed for cash, have constructed their case for closing down institutional provisions and turning people into the community to receive the caring individual attention that institutions have been unable to provide (Baldwin, 1985). The Barclay (1982), Griffiths (1988), and Wagner (1988) Reports have formally endorsed these expectations for community based social work and ignored the implications of sexism and racism in their proposals.

Community Organisation

This form of community work promotes community interests by improving co-ordination between various welfare agencies. It aims to avoid wasting resources by ending the duplication of efforts, allowing interagency pooling of facilities and managing facilities better. Community groups are expected to be strengthened in securing their objectives through such initiatives. The community worker is usually a paid 'expert' male professional with organisational knowledge who gives direct advice to the people who are being helped. The professional advice proferred is perceived as paternalistic by residents and does not threaten the *status quo*. It is often conducive to helping those in power retain their privileges and control over resources by containing working-class anger and channelling it through approved structures (Dearlove, 1974). Many community participation exercises on town plans and road schemes, flounder against this type of community intervention for it gives people power lacking substance. Community organisation became popularised as part of a corporate approach to welfare issues. It formed a useful tool in the hands of management concerned with making the best use of its resources, when these were being rationed. Moreover, the allocation of resources on this basis ignores the specific needs of women and black people. As we shall see below, this model has been used extensively in Britain since the 1960s.

Community Development

Community work formulated on the community development model attempts to help people acquire the self-help skills necessary for them to improve their lot. It relies on educational processes initiated by community workers using either a directive or a non-directive approach (Batten, 1967). The community worker is usually a man who helps people learn by working on problems they have identified. He is typically a paid professional interested in reforming the system through social engineering. His work is usually based on residential areas which the state has targetted for 'community work' intervention to help overcome their social problems. The presence of such problems is presumed to indicate a backwardness on the part of inhabitants who are believed to lack the skills necessary for enriching their community. This view legitimises bringing in expert 'outsiders' to provide the leadership necessary for mobilising people around specific issues and organising them to improve the situation. Action is collective and acknowledges the possibility of conflict if opponents prove unresponsive to the group's demands. However, negotiation and discussion are the main tools used in the organising process. Protracted struggle may indicate that it is necessary to change the system, at which point, community development may turn into community action. The community development model may draw heavily on women to provide the grassroots support and resources a project requires during its implementation. Black people have found this model used in their communities to integrate them more thoroughly into the capitalist system in subordinate positions (Ng, 1988).

Class Based Community Action

Community work organised according to this model is usually militant, bringing people lacking power together to reduce their powerlessness and increase their effectiveness. Claimants Unions are an example of community groups utilising this model (Rose, 1973). Though class oriented community action usually begins at a local level, it is often extended to regional and other levels to maximise its effectiveness. It uses conflict, direct action, confrontation and negotiation to achieve its ends. The distinction between the community worker and the rest of the group is usually blurred, as the community worker tries to become an active member of that community and work with others on an egalitarian basis. As these groups engage in conflict, members rapidly become community activists. The community group's objectives center on exposing the contradictions on which society is based and shifting the existing allocation of power and resources. Thus, class oriented community action is about social change. The

11

Community Development Projects in Britain started out as community organisation/community development models but some quickly became community action oriented, thus setting themselves up in conflict with the state (Community Development Projects Working Group, 1977), prompting the state, as funder, to close the more problematic Projects, despite having earlier agreed to extend their funding. Class oriented community action has traditionally been very masculist in its theory and practice. Most of the paid community work posts were held by white men who played key roles in identifying the processes as well as the targets for action. Their method of behaviour and their analyses of social problems often alienated both women (Dixon et al, 1982) and black people involved in these projects (Ohri and Manning, 1982). But drawing on the women's movement and black liberation struggles, women and black people respectively developed their own forms of community action to cater specifically for their own needs.

Feminist Community Action

Feminists active in the women's liberation movement have challenged masculist community work on both theoretical and practical grounds. They have taken traditional community work's concern with issues affecting people's daily lives in the community and its commitment to resolving disputes through collective action and transformed its theory and practice. This has been done by focusing on gender as a central feature of collective action that takes place in the community and harnessing its powers to promote social change which will foster gender equality (Wilson, 1977b; Marchant and Wearing, 1986; Dominelli and McLeod, 1989). Feminist community action has transcended the boundaries of traditional community work by challenging fundamentally the nature of capitalist patriarchal social relations between men and women, women and the state, and adults and children through action which begins in the routine activities of daily life. By picking up on the specific needs of women as people previously excluded in community work, feminists have developed theory and practice, new understandings of the concept 'community' and revealed the political nature of the social relations embedded within it. At the same time, they exposed the politicised nature of power relations between men and women in society more generally (Adamson et al, 1988).

In highlighting the problematic nature of the concept 'the community' from a woman's point of view, feminist community workers have revealed the extent to which it relied on exploiting women's energies for the 'common good' (Finch and Groves, 1983) and questioned prevailing definitions of what constitutes appropriate subjects for community action (Curno et al., 1982).

12

They also challenged the division of society into the private domestic sphere outside of public scrutiny which encompasses women's place in the community and the male dominated sphere of social, political and economic life. This delineation is accepted by traditional and radical community workers alike (see Leonard, 1975; Bailey and Brake, 1975). Feminists' redefinition of private lives and concern with women's emotional fulfillment as well as their physical needs enabled feminists to focus on domestic violence, child sexual abuse and other hidden forms of injustice (see Mayo, 1977; Curno et al, 1982; Dominelli and McLeod, 1989) and makes gender the basis of a dialectical process of organisation (Brandwein, 1987). In tackling issues community workers previously shunned, feminists have developed new methods of organisation, for example, consciousness-raising (Dreifus, 1973); redefined power relationships and focused on sharing power according to 'win-win' principles in which everyone gained from conflict resolution rather than someone losing to the more powerful (Brandwein, 1987); highlighted the need for the positive appraisal of the contribution women make to society (Janssen-Jurret, 1982); made connections between different responsibilities women had to carry (Dominelli and McLeod, 1989) and; worked for forms of community work enhancing the welfare of women, men and children (Marchant and Wearing, 1986; Brook and Davis, 1985; Dominelli and McLeod, 1989). Feminists have also sought to deal with the impact of different forms of oppression, for example, classism, racism, ageism, and the divisions these create amongst women in the context of their own practice (Davis, 1989; Lorde, 1984; Bryan et al., 1985). Feminist community action became a vehicle through which feminist ideology, theory and practice elaborated the feminist view that the 'personel is political' (Dreifus, 1973); 'politics is personal' (Ungerson, 1987) and 'sisterhood is universal' (Adamson et al. 1988; Morgan, 1984).

Community Action from a Black Perspective

The failure of community work organisations to address racism as a specific issue hindered the development of services meeting black people's particular needs and compelled black people to develop their own forms of community action (Mullard, 1973; Ohri and Manning, 1982). Criticising the inappropriateness of community workers operating on the colourblind approach and, making the struggle for racial equality central to their work, black community activists created a range of provisions to meet the needs of black people which simultaneously addressed the problems which social divisions created in their organisations (Sondhi, 1982). Their activities have included establishing anti-racist and anti-ageist provisions for their elders (ASRA, 1981); campaigns and networks to support individuals and groups tackling state institutionalised racism, particularly in social security and immigration regulations (Sondhi, 1982); and care (Small, 1984). Black women have also created their own community groups to examine issues and develop facilities appropriate for them. These have included establishing black women's refuges (Guru, 1987), health care networks (Malek, 1985) and child care provisions (Farrah, 1986). Black women have also played a significant role in developing feminist theory and practice (Bryan *et al*, 1985; Hooks, 1984; Davis, 1989; Bhavani and Coulson, 1986; Wilson, 1986; Dominelli and McLeod, 1989; Barrett and McIntosh, 1985). This has been particularly evident in their critique of the racism inherent in white feminist community work practice. Anti-racist feminist community work has drawn inspiration from both black and white women committed to empowering people in developing facilities aimed at eliminating both racial and gender inequality. These have eschewed prioritising one form of oppression over another and required that all types of inequality be tackled simultaneously (Hooks, 1984; Dominelli and McLeod, 1989; Davis, 1989).

Chapter 1

A Place of One's Own
The Feminist Challenge to
Traditional Community Work

Community work as a method of organisation has had a number of different objectives. It has been used to control populations as well as to spark off revolutionary change (Mayo, 1975). The use of community work in controlling insurgent populations is evident in Northern Ireland (Griffiths, 1974a). The mass campaigns that created the *barefoot doctor* system in China during the Cultural Revolution initiated revolutionary changes in health care delivery (Horn, 1969). Similarly, the use of 'speak bitterness meetings' in the early 1950s in China were crucial elements in community action aimed at challenging male violence against women (Hinton, 1966). In between these two extremes, community work has been used to foster the formation of local caring networks, encourage communities to take responsibility for their plight, and provide work, paid and unpaid, for individuals and groups. Community work has also been an important vehicle through which the voluntary sector organised self-help initiatives drawing on women's traditional skills to support hard-pressed individuals and supplement resources provided by the state, for example, Meals-on-Wheels; challenge the adequacy of state services, for example, provisions for elders and their carers; and develop new ways of organising, for example, feminist consciousness-raising groups.

State sponsored community work and voluntary sector initiatives, particularly those lacking a feminist stamp, have adopted community work models such as community care, community organisation and community development. State sponsored initiatives have used similar models, but their aims and objectives have occasionally differed substantially from those advanced by voluntary organisations. The development of community action as *the form* of radical community work in the late 1960s and early 1970s has marked one such point. Community action has challenged community workers' commitment to reforming the *status quo* by suggesting that the basic organisation of society and its distribution of power and resources were responsible for creating declining communities and required widescale social change to remedy

15

(Community Development Projects Working Group, 1975). Changing society became a key objective of community action. However, community action in its early days was preoccupied with economic issues and housing and had little to say about women's role in the community and their contribution to its activities. Elisabeth Wilson, (1977b), laments the failure of radical community work to take on board the realisation of gender equality despite the existence of a women's movement which had highlighted connections between women and the community. She wrote:

> 'Community workers . . . have not even begun to come to grips with these problems for the simple reason that they have yet to reach a stage at which they understand that women suffer from a specific form of oppression'. (Wilson 1977b.7.)

Contributing to this failure was the tendency of community politics to veer towards hierarchy and welfarism because professionals with expertise, knowledge and the regulations, understanding or opportune moments and access to resources were able to acquire power over community group members lacking these attributes (Wilson, 1977b).

Feminist community work has developed partly in reaction to the invisibility of women in both traditional and radical community work. The women's liberation movement has underpinned feminist initiatives with women in the community and made possible the development of a form of community action which it could call its own. Feminist community workers have launched a challenge which transcends the demands of radical community activists. They are calling for a more fundamental change than that presaged by a simple redistribution of power and resources between classes in society and are insisting that gender oppression be placed on the agenda (Wilson and Weir, 1986). Moreover, feminists have demanded that the techniques, aims, and objectives of community workers reflect egalitarian principles as part and parcel of their work rather than being left as an item to be realised at the end of the process (Wandor, 1972). Feminist community work has differentiated itself from community work undertaken by women insofar as it has, albeit somewhat imperfectly, challenged existing social relations by aiming to eradicate gender oppression and promote egalitarianism in its activities.

In this chapter we examine types of community work in vogue in the 1960s, the impact of radical community action upon it, and the theoretical developments and practical innovations introduced by feminist community workers. We will also consider the relationships between these different forms of community work and the state, and the place of women within them. In the course of doing so, the centrality of women's action in community work processes and how their place in the community has been circumscribed by their being defined as mothers, wives and daughters rather than as individuals in their own right is revealed.

16

In other words, the chapter will highlight feminists' challenge to patriarchal social relations through the medium of feminist community action.

Community Work and the British State

Economic crisis in the late 1950s as the post-war boom of the 'you never had it so good' era drew to a close, produced social problems which shattered the complacency of the British public. The 'rediscovery of poverty' in the early 1960s, a growing black activist movement resisting racial oppression, the 'breakdown of the family' and the rise in juvenile crime became major areas of concern for the British state and its legislators during the 1960s. Both Tory and Labour governments worried about the failure of the welfare state to meet the needs of the workforce on the one hand and those of capital on the other. The state commissioned numerous reports, including the Milner Holland Report on London's Housing, the Ingleby Report on Children and Young Persons, the Plowden Report on Primary Education, and the Seebohm Report on the Personal Social Services, which all pointed to the failure of the welfare state in meeting working class needs. These reports pointed out that the country was dotted with areas of 'special need' or 'pockets of deprivation' requiring comprehensive policies to eradicate the poverty ensconced within them. The identification of the problem in these terms legitimised the belief that generally, British people were doing well; the welfare state had succeeded in eliminating the harsh realities of income inequality. The presence of 'pockets of deprivation' was explained by pathologising individuals and communities. Limited areas of disadvantage existed because people did not know their rights and how to obtain services from the state; could not be bothered to work for their living; or had something wrong with them personally – disability, lack of education, preventing them from grasping control of their lives. Thus, the poor were blamed for their poverty. Pathologising the poor meant that social planners did not have to address issues of structural change, but could focus on tinkering with the outer margins of social organisation (Community Development Project, 1977b).

Blaming the victims of poverty for their plight was also apparent in other reports such as *Children, Family and Young Offenders* and *Children in Trouble* which held the increase in divorce and single parent families responsible for the social problems enumerated above. Working mothers were perceived as precipitating juvenile delinquency by being absent from home. The media deplored the high number of deprived 'latch-key' children produced by wage earning mothers. Working class families were castigated for failing to provide society with the 'law-abiding' citizens required. Besides castigating victims, the state sought to reduce welfare costs by making more effective use of its material

17

and human resources, and introducing corporate management techniques into a reorganised local state.

The state's strategy in tackling social problems was two pronged. One prong relied on traditional population control methods such as strengthening the 'law and order' apparatuses – the police, magistrate's courts, prisons, and the probation service (Bunyan, 1977). It also sought to control the workforce by restricting trade union activity through legislation foreshadowed in *In Place of Strife* and implemented under the 1971 Industrial Relations Act; and controlling immigration under the Commonwealth Immigration Act of 1962 which began regulating the size of the 'external' reserve army of labour provided by black people (Castles and Kosack, 1972). As these measures on their own were inadequate, the state's other prong aimed at a 'softer' approach which secured the consent of the governed to their domination. The 'soft' approach concentrated on the development of social structures appropriate to the task. Community work was an indispensable element in this strategy. The structures initiated under this policy included the Community Relations Commission, the Race Relations Board, (these two bodies were subsumed by the Commission for Racial Equality in 1976), the Urban Aid Programme, the Community Development Projects, later replaced by the Urban Deprivation Unit, and the Comprehensive Community Programmes. The Urban Aid Programme was subsequently altered to the Inner Area Programme which included the Inner Area Partnership Schemes and Free Enterprise Zones. The state's attempts to simultaneously satisfy the needs of both labour and capital were contradictory, for promoting the interests of one could only occur at the expense of the other. The state's strategy however, was compatible with the social democratic ideology, then firing the imaginations of the populace and legislators alike.

The government initially responded to the demand that deprived areas be given additional resources by discriminating in favour of areas with the greatest needs and fewest resources by the introduction of a 'needs' element in the allocation of funding through the Rate Support Grant. Local authorities receiving this money were responsible for distributing it locally. Their emphasis on areas of 'special need' was conducive to the employment of community workers charged with co-ordinating aspects of local authority work in the targetted areas. The concentration of black people in decaying inner cities and increasing black unrest following racist attacks on them in Nottinghill in 1958, yielded a government response parallelling the one described above. Community relations officers were duly appointed to deal with the racial dimension of deprivation, under a remit which incorporated black activists and pathologised black communities (Mullard, 1973). Meanwhile, the state was busy cultivating the view that racism was the product of the presence of too many black people in Britain and introducing immigration controls to contain their numbers (Sivanandan, 1976; Mullard, 1973). As with deprived white communities, black communities were also pathologised and blamed for their plight. However, black people also had to deal with the impact of racist immigration legislation which caused them hardship by denying admission to their kin, splitting their families, and excluding them from welfare state services through regulations which were racist in their impact, for example the residency requirement for access to council housing (Bryan *et al*, 1985).

The Urban Aid Programme (UAP) was launched in 1968 in the aftermath of Enoch Powell's 'Rivers of Blood' speech in Birmingham. This outburst by a government minister lent legitimacy to the view that harmonious race relations could be acquired only by controlling the numbers of black settlers in Britain and endorsed institutionalised racism which in turn made individual racism respectable (CCCS, 1982). The UAP was based on a philosophy of a 'social pathology' theory of poverty and a strategy of action drawing on lessons learnt during the American War on Poverty Programme (Community Development Project, 1977b). The Home Office was responsible for the UAP and contributed 75% of funding for approved projects. The local authority supporting the project's application contributed the remaining 25%. In theory, this provided an avenue through which additional money could be channelled into needy areas. In practice, this did not happen. UAP monies came out of the general allocation in the Rate Support Grant, though placed in a 'Special Grant' category. The amount of money allocated to the UAP was small: £60–65 million. However, only £43–45 million was actually spent. The failure rate of applicants was high: 5 applications were rejected for every one approved (Community Development Project, 1977b).

The government provided indices of multiple deprivation which allowed local authorities to assess 'need' when supporting bids. These were:

* deficiencies in the environment, particularly housing;
* overcrowding;
* higher than average family size;
* persistent unemployment;
* a high proportion of children in trouble or in need of care; and
* a high number of children requiring free school meals.

These factors did not address the specific needs of either black people or women. Bridges (1975) argues that the UAP was developed, not to attend to people's needs but, as a form of social control aimed at penetrating communities, particularly black communities, for more effective policing.

The Community Development Projects (CDPs) were introduced in 1969 under the UAP. Originally, these were experimental community based action-research projects with an intended five year life span through which the government hoped to incorporate voluntary and community groups. The Home Office established twelve CDPs, each having an action team undertaking community work and a university-based research team monitoring the action team's activities. Although CDPs were locally based, the Home Office maintained ultimate control over their development by sitting on their management committees and approving funding for specific groups or pieces of work. Local authorities maintained day-to-day control over the CDPs' programme of work through their management committee and by authorising the release of social action funds for approved projects. The CDPs work, the government hoped, would;

> improve the efficiency of local government by co-ordinating service delivery and avoiding the unnecessary replication of services; affect local and central government policies through its research; and encourage local residents' participation in policy formulation and service delivery through the establishment of self-help groups.

These aims reveal a piecemeal approach to social problems predicated on the assumption that the system was basically sound. A similar tack was evident in the Seebohm Report's attempts to improve local authority service delivery and the Skeffington Report's promotion of citizen participation. The piecemeal perspective on social change resonated with the central state's desire to spread its resources over the largest number of people whilst retaining general control over their direction on the ground. These initiatives were consistent with the principles of corporate management, or the cost-effective use of resources under centralised control. They also enabled the state to draw on community work for their implementation in the field.

However, the contradictions inherent in the UAP/CDP proposals were soon exposed. CDP's work demonstrated the inadequacy of the social pathology theory of poverty whilst Sir Keith Joseph was trying to re-assert its validity through his 'cycle of transmitted deprivation' speeches during 1972–74. These sought to intensify the blame heaped on single parent families by arguing that their poverty was the outcome of deficiencies which reappeared in generation after generation. It was another twist in the screw holding women responsible for society's ills. CDPs' work also put paid to the theory that middle level mismanagement was responsible for the welfare state's failure to meet local needs. Instead of pathologising individuals and communities. CDPs' analysis and work increasingly demonstrated the structural basis of poverty (Community Development Project, 1977a and b). CDPs revealed that declining local economies caused by capital seeking more profitable areas for exploitation, including those located in the Third World, caused poverty. Furthermore, they indicated that poverty was supported through social structures which perpetuated society's unequal distribution of power and resources. *CDPs message, the poor are essential if capitalism is to flourish, was not one which either local or central state wished to broadcast.* The state prematurely ended CDPs by immediately closing particularly problematic ones (for example, Cleator Moore, Batley) whilst starving the remainder of funds and ultimately closing the lot. The relatively weak power base of the CDPs meant that there was little successful opposition to the state's moves. In the meantime, the central state which had been monitoring closely the results being achieved by CDPs, had already established structures which could continue community work along more contolled lines (Community Development Project, 1977b).

The organisation of CDPs produced its own internal contradictions. Gender inequality was prevalent. Women community workers and secretaries were expected to make the tea and undertake the servicing work in the teams. Additionally, it was apparent that women community workers were also receiving less pay than male community workers, and holding lower level jobs, regardless of their qualifications. No account was taken of women workers dual career burden in the organisation of the work.

The promotion of the Working Women's Charter by the labour and women's movements in the early 1970s, encouraged a group of CDP women endorsing the Charter's aims to meet together to examine CDPs failure to address the issue of gender inequality within its own ranks. The late Jeanette Mitchell, Penny Remfry and myself were amongst those who attended the few meetings that examined this matter before CDPs, including the Central Office, were disbanded. The difficulties besetting us in forming a national organisation of CDP women were many. Our meetings were on top of those related to the work we were undertaking in the community, although the irony of ignoring gender inequality in CDPs whilst we were trying to eradicate it in the community did strike us. The work of uncovering the specifics of women's position in CDPs (for example, examining pay scales, the position of secretaries, the roles women occupied) had to be completed on top of a full day's work. Additionally, as CDPs were dispersed nationally, and the number of women in any one team small, it was both time consuming and expensive for us to travel regularly to one location to meet even if it were rotated.

At the beginning, CDPs work with women in the community followed traditional lines (Remfry, 1979). Women were organised into women's groups to deal with issues concerning them as mothers, for example, childcare provisions. There was no attempt to involve men in these activities and make such work relevant to

21

them. Women who were supported in improving their position at work, for example, obtaining union recognition in workplaces predominantly hiring women, found no consideration given to their specific needs as women workers, for example, taking account of the dual career burden they carried, timing meetings to facilitate their participation, providing childcare facilities to encourage attendance. CDPs primary concern was the alleviation of poverty. Its analyses of poverty did not include an understanding of the gendered impact of poverty. In these circumstances, the conclusion that CDPs related to women on a gender blind basis and did little to challenge women's oppression as women should astound no one. However, feminist community work was beginning to prosper in certain CDPs towards the end of their active life, for example, North Tyneside. Issues such as domestic violence and the needs of women workers as women began being addressed. Some of these initiatives have survived the demise of CDPs.

The CDPs record on confronting racism is only marginally better. Several CDPs working with black communities, for example, Saltley and Batley, attempted to tackle this issue and were able to expose many institutionalised racist practices, for example, the 'redlining' of black communities for mortgage purposes (Community Development Project, 1977c). 'Redlining' meant that building societies considered the areas 'high risk' and refused applicants loans for houses located in them. However, racism permeated social relations between black community workers and their white CDP colleagues. When employed, black people were usually hired at the lower levels, although the work they were expected to undertake was more complex than that of white workers. Additionally, black workers found that the responsibility for eliminating racism in the community and within CDP was often dumped on their shoulders.

In working with black women, white women community workers' attempts to counter the dynamics of racism and sexism were often mishandled, despite their commitment to being sensitive to the needs of black women and their position in the community. A certain amount of benevolent paternalism pervaded their relationships, for example, the assumption that Mirpuri or Gujarati women needed their intervention and mediation with the black men controlling their communities to form women's groups. CDPs may have held a radical reputation, but it certainly was not merited in terms of their contributions to eliminating the oppression of women and black people.

The Community Programmes Department was established in 1971. It followed a community organisation model of community work and launched a number of programmes which unlike those originating under UAP were aimed at concentrating resources in small areas, for example, the Neighbourhood Schemes. Community

22

Programmes continued focusing on co-ordinating activities and improving service delivery, but dropped the earlier emphasis on local participation. Liverpool and Teeside had the only two Neighbourhood Schemes finally launched. Women were called to contribute their resources by providing informal care. The competition between different community groups for scarce state funding was evident in the financing of this scheme. The £300,000 allocated to it came from the Urban Aid budget.

The Department of the Environment entered the arena through the Inner Area Studies which reported in 1973, at the cost of £1.3 million. Of this money, 75% was provided by the Department of Environment, and 25% by the local authorities involved. Oldham, Rotherham, and Sunderland had the first projects under the Inner Area Studies. These were followed by schemes in Birmingham, Liverpool and London which considered the role of local authorities and local councillors in eliminating urban deprivation. However, their work constituted a bureaucratic professional exercise undertaken by private management and economic planning consultants rather than grassroots oriented community work. Their arrangements addressed neither the needs of women and black people nor their exclusion from the political process.

The proliferation of 'community work' initiatives, including some not mentioned here, worried the Treasury who wanted to contain such expenditure and ensure CDPs' experience of community workers going their own way was not repeated. The Urban Deprivation Unit (UDU) was created in 1973 to co-ordinate all programmes dealing with urban deprivation. Their ventures were to rely more on community organisation models of community work and operate on mangerialist lines without grassroots involvement (CDP, 1977b) The UDU formulated the Comprehensive Community Programmes (CCP) which adopted community organisation models of community work for small areas of need. CCPs aimed to coordinate all existing action on deprivation in a locality and highlight gaps in existing programmes. Those areas found to be *most* in need would be eligible for funding, others would not. This strategy did not appeal to local authorities who felt that their whole jurisdiction needed resources if a particular needy area were to be helped. However, only four pilot CCPs involving 'deprivation' experts in the corporate management and committee machinery of local authorities were launched. These targetted Bradford, Gateshead, Wandsworth, and the Wirral. The UDU also set up projects in Greater London deprived areas – Spitalfields, Tower Hamlets, and Henley Road, Islington.

The Department of the Environment added its own projects known as the Area Management Trials. These projects, launched in Dudley and Haringay provided an area manager to co-ordinate policies and act as an access point for local groups. The main aim of these new urban deprivation projects was to ensure that

23

resources were managed more effectively and left little scope for direct community participation. Endorsing community organisation principles of action, these relied on 'experts' issuing directives to 'passive' communities. The net effect of these policies was to curtail public participation in their localites and 'depoliticise' community issues, turning them into neutral technical problems which could be most appropriately handled by technicians bringing their expertise to bear on them. Women and black people, rarely found in managerial positions, had little input in the formulation of these directives.

By 1976, the UDUs' initiatives were formalised in Labour's *Policies for Inner Cities*. This set the stage for the Inner Area Partnership Schemes (IAPS) which have remained strategic in the state's handling of urban poverty. Stressing 'self-help' and community development, IAPS accepted that economic decline is responsible for urban deprivation to a certain degree. state intervention has stressed the provision of resources through a partnership between the local and the central state. IAPS aims to attract private industry into its designated areas through special tax concessions, subsidies and publicly provided infrastructures such as roads and communications networks. IAPS' structure effectively excludes women and black people who can rarely muster the resources necessarty for launching entrepreneurial initiatives. IAPS also annoyed local authorities denied partnership status despite the high incidence of deprivation within their borders as the lack of designation deprived them of access to urban aid funds. Central government control over IAPS ensured that funds were disproportionately allocated to schemes which followed a traditional service oritentation at the expense of community action and housing action projects. Radical community action initiatives in Leeds, Leicester and Liverpool were particularly hard hit by the government's policy (Armstrong, 1977). Consequently, feminist initiatives and community action from a black perspective secured little of the funding made available through IAPS.

The Free Enterprise Zones (FEZ) initiated by the Conservative government in 1980 to encourage private industry's investment in inner city areas extended the state's concessions to private firms and eliminated many of the planning regulations commercial enterprises disliked. Women, largely excluded from the 'cut and thrust' of free enterprise played virtually no part in firms' investment decisions. FEZ enabled firms to penetrate declining communities without being accountable for the casualties they created en route. IAPS and FEZ have had a limited impact in stemming inner city decay. In fact, the rebellion of young black people in London, Liverpool, Birmingham, Leeds and Leicester in the summer of 1981 was testimony to the failure of IAPS and FEZ to meet their needs. Since then, rising unemployment, increasing economic decline in Britain's inner cities and the increase of racist attacks have demonstrated the bankruptcy of the various free enterprise initiatives through which the state has sought to revitalise inner cities. Even its strategy of developing a sizeable black middle class along the lines of the American experience has failed to reduce poverty in the inner cities. The FEZ strategy was not intended to directly tackle either racial or gender inequality and it excluded residents from its decision making processes.

Whilst the central and local state were forming a partnership aimed at encouraging economic reconstruction through private investments, their welfare activities were being used to mitigate the damage done to people who were thrown on the 'scrapheap' through economic decline. However, this occurred within the context of severely curtailed welfare expenditures (Iliffe, 1985; Loney, 1986). The growing number of economic casualties stretched these limited resources. Government's response culminating in the 1986 Social Security Act excluded various client groups from coverage, for example, sixteen to eighteen year olds from supplementary benefits, women from the previously universal maternity grant, and all client groups seeking income support through the abolition of special needs payments (LSCC, 1986).

Besdies depriving women of benefits, as had happened under earlier revisions to the social security system, the government's welfare strategy called upon women to provide unpaid informal caring and low paid welfare work. At the same time, the state sought to further limit its commitments to open-ended welfare expenditures by forcing people off welfare and into low paid work. The role of the Manpower Services Commission, now the National Training Board, was crucial in providing 'training' and 'retraining' schemes in partnership with employers and trade unions, to absorb the casualties of deindustrialisation and refit them for new employment opportunities (Finn, 1985). With the exception of low paid part-time work attracting women (Segal, 1987), few job opportunities materialised for either men or women and unemployment levels remain high. At one point training resources were rationed by excluding married women from the Community Programme – an initiative aimed at attracting the long-term unemployed into temporary work. Since many projects under this initiative were part-time community work programmes, this ruling had serious implications for women. Meanwhile, the state was declaring the costs of providing an increasing number of people with social security, housing, education and health provisions to be too great within its existing framework of priorities.

The public expenditure cuts severely affected welfare state provision in housing, education, social security, health and personal social services and marked the central state's decision to restrict its commitments to filling 'a bottomless pit of need'. Limiting public expenditure was the state's response to imposing efficiency in the allocation of resources upon the welfare bureaucracy. Consequently, the government had to develop strategies which would bring in additional resources at no extra cost. Drawing on the voluntary sector, women's unpaid domestic care and private enterprise were attractive for this reason (Iliffe, 1985). The state's twin needs to be both controlling and cost effective surfaced anew at the local level, exacerbating the detrimental impact of industrial decline on individuals, particularly women and black people who felt the impact of withdrawn services and poverty most. At such a juncture, community work as community development becomes useful in rationing resources. The use of community work for such purposes had been facilitated by the retreat of state funded community action critical of the local state's responses to deprived areas, exemplified by the CDP experience. The departure of CDPs had left a vacuum which the state filled by firstly, maintaining community workers in voluntary settings using 'self-help' principles and secondly, employing them in statutory settings where it could directly control their labour process. Good Neighbour Schemes, community care schemes, voluntary self-help initiatives and the 'patch' system of community social work have clearly legitimised community work within such parameters (Wolfenden, 1977; Barclay, 1982; Griffiths, 1988; Wagner, 1988; Hadley et al., 1987). The closure of residential homes and day-centres has pushed their users into communities with few other provisions catering for their needs. The 'cuts' in welfare services for older people, the disabled and handicapped promoted the establishment of 'self-help' groups aimed at cushioning the effects of the withdrawal of such resources. Alongside self-help organisations, private entrepreneurs and unpaid domestic provisions provided by women in the home have reduced the resulting gaps. The burden of care forced onto women, in both their unwaged and waged capacities, has added to their existing load of caring. Although the state makes it sound like it provides the bulk of care for older people and children, this is not the case. Most older persons and children are cared for privately and with virtually no state support by women in their homes (Higgins, 1989).

The local state had been exploring the use of community workers within social services departments since the Seebohm reorganisation in the late 1960s. Local authorities have found they can control these workers performance of their tasks by tightening the boundaries in which they work. state employed community workers have been used to: demonstrate that the state is still concerned about the effects of deprivation on working-class people; collect information on how working-class communities cope with the onslaught of economic decline and the fragmentation of their social life; and develop more efficient policies for deploying limited state resources.

The Seebohm Report (1968) had laid the basis for a community work dimension in social services through the concept of the area team (Leissner and Joslin, 1974). According to Seebohm, area teams were to be locality based to facilitate the development of a 'comprehensive area team approach' and provide 'an effective family social service'. The teams, through experience and training would become 'skilled at working with and in the community'. This advice followed the realisation that 60% of social work cases involved low income and bad housing (Seebohm, 1968). Such reasoning underpinned the impetus for 'patch' based neighbourhood work within area teams. The opening provided by Seebohm was widened in the Barclay Report (1982) which encouraged local authorities to develop community social work. Community social work was intended to increase social workers effectiveness in the community and reduce costs by enabling workers to cover more people more effectively with the same amount of resources (Cockburn, 1977). The Wagner Report (1988) endorsed these proposals and advocated the widespread use of community care as the way in which social services departments could make their services more relevant to users' needs (Ungerson, 1987). The Griffiths Report (1988) assumed women's labour would underpin community based health care. None of these Reports included the unpaid work of women in their costings. Yet, women bear a personal cost in terms of a fraught existence and foregone opportunities by putting their labour at the disposal of others (Ashurst and Hall, 1989). Neither did these Reports acknowledge the centrality of women's unpaid contribution to the viability of their proposed schemes. These Reports confirm Elisabeth Wilson's (1982) views that the word 'community' 'is an ideological portmeanteau word for a reactionary, conservative ideology that oppresses women by silently confining them to the private sphere without so much as even mentioning them.'

The forms of community work endorsed by Barclay (1982), Wagner (1988) and Griffiths (1988) could potentially employ large numbers of community workers in servicing activities defined and controlled by local authorities. These would break community workers' potential to mobilise people by focusing on job functions emphasising their roles in elaborating government policy and managing local authorities' limited financial resources and buildings. However, there is space for manoeuvre within this restricted position (London–Edinburgh Weekend Return Group, 1979). Community workers' use of it hinges on the nature of their compliance with their job descriptions and their ability to secure the consent of residents to intervene in their lives in progressive directions. The extent to which community workers can creatively utilise these spaces also depends on their ability to organise a strong power base amongst their constituents. Their position is a contradictory one full of potential and limitations.

Community Work, Corporate Management and Restructuring Hierarchical Institutions

The development of community work in the public sector has also been influenced by corporate management playing a significant role in the restructuring of the labour process and reorganisation of social services (Cockburn, 1977). Corporate management in the public sector has relied on adopting techniques developed in industry to make the most effective use of labour power and resoucres by shifting the balance of power on the shop-floor towards management. The drive for efficiency in the public sector has been interpreted as the need to cut waste and unnecessary expenditure by returning the responsibility for care to 'the family', that is to women (Glazer, 1988). The public expenditure cuts have accelerated both the implementation and effects of corporate management in social services. Corporate decision-making has increased managerial control over day-to-day decision making in areas which once resided within the realms of professional autonomy, for example, managerial directives on the handling of child abuse. From a community action perspective, such erosion of professional power would be more easily countenanced if it had empowered service users. But, this has not happened. Management's control of the labour process has strengthened the hand of bureaucratic experts, fragmenting the labour process and transformed the nature of decision-making. Decisions about the allocation of resources are no longer political questions but technical ones. Instead of focusing on the political question of *why* resources have been allocated in particular ways, workers have got bogged down in answering the technical question of *how* to allocate available resources, given certain constraints. The implications of this for women have been quite serious. Management making the decisions has meant primarily men making the decisions (Howe, 1986; Coyle and Skinner, 1988). Many of them have never worked with clients and have little appreciation of the complex realities social workers handle daily whilst their space for manoeuvre has been whittled away. Moreover, losing the right to shape working plans with clients has made women frontline workers party to bureaucratic and remote forms of service delivery which have increasingly alienated users.

The absence of a corporate management structure has been used by the voluntary sector to claim it has greater freedom in developing more progressive forms of practice (Ng, 1988). Viewing the voluntary sector as autonomous ignores the reality of the constraints insecure funding places on it. The state has used its funding of voluntary initiatives to integrate them more securely into capitalist social relations (Cockburn, 1977; Ng, 1988). Funding structures the relationship between the state and voluntary organisations, legitimates certain activities whilst excluding others, and alters the internal relationships and dynamics of voluntary groups (Ng, 1988). These effects are particularly problematic for groups attempting to work in non-hierarchical ways (Ng, 1988). However, the women's movement and black community activists have developed autonomous alternative forms of practice by drawing largely on their own resources, for example, Incest Survivor Groups and refuges (Binney *et al.*, 1981; Mama, 1989). However these provisions have often been exploited by statutory services who have used them to cover recognised gaps in services which they continue to neglect (Gilroy, 1987; Scottish Women's Aid Federation, 1980).

Organising Tips

Constraints of Hierarchy

1) What are these?
2) What action is required to overcome them?
3) What resources are required to implement the action?
4) What support groups/alliances are necessary?

Community Action within a Social Services Setting – the 'Patch' System

Social workers' growing disillusionment with their ability to offer clients a meaningful service in the context of the public expenditure cuts and the dismantling of the welfare state, has increased their interest in the possibilities contained within community work (Hadley and Hatch, 1981). Ironically, this concern on the social workers' part has coincided with the state's desire to improve delivery of the personal social services to the community without increasing costs and contain community action within acceptable parameters. The state has tried to meet its concerns by employing community workers within social services departments to work a 'patch' under a defined remit. These community workers, technically part of the social services team, often operate in the community and restrict their contact with their district team. 'Patch' workers tend to have little impact on the work of office-based social workers, although as community workers they can be aware of residents' hostility and frustration with the inadequate responses to their plight offered by social services departments. Separation of the community work and the social work component in district teams remains the norm. However, several local authorities have pioneered the integration of community work techniques with those of social casework, and switched teams over to the 'patch' system, for example, Birmingham, Nottingham and Wakefield. These have sought to increase community participation in planning services (Cooper, 1980).

Establishing a 'patch' system is problematic. Opponents to the system need to be convinced of its viability. They can be ensconced anywhere in the social services department, beginning with the members of the social services committee, right down to the district teams. Before the programme can be enacted, a lengthy process of educating people and convincing them of the advantages of the 'patch' must be undertaken. The educative process requires the development of links with councillors, senior and middle-management, fieldworkers, and trade unions. Councillors' support for a 'patch' scheme can facilitate its realisation. They can work to commit the social services committee to fostering the district team's right to engage in innovative and preventative work rather than merely responding to crises. Convincing councillors of the appropriateness of such action is not easy. The process may be protracted, and the final outcome may simply be the endorsement of the 'patch' system by one or two councillors (see Cockburn, 1977).

Obtaining trade union support is also important. Trade unions can put pressure on employers through negotiations and/or industrial action and shift their stance from opposing social workers' proposals to favouring them (Joyce et al., 1987). Union solidarity can also be used to protect workers' career prospects in the event of a dispute over the implementation of the 'patch' system. Middle management's support for the proposal can facilitate its progress through social services bureaucratic machinery.

The 'patch' system was initially envisaged as a means whereby social services could become more relevant to the needs of users. Rather than becoming a means whereby deprived working-class communities can procure additional resources, it can easily become a mechanism through which the community becomes co-opted by the social services department drawing on existing community resources and is used to compensate for deficiencies in service delivery. One reason for this unbalanced relationship is that social workers intent on the 'patch' system focus more on securing employer support for the scheme than involving the community. Its passage through the social services department proceeds along professional and trade union channels. Once approval is formally granted, the 'patch' system is presented to the community as a package on which it is briefly consulted. The community is subsequently asked to ratify the 'patch' plan by using it and providing the additional human and material resources it requires. 'Patch' systems have been used in a variety of settings to offer a range of services. For instance, 'patch' systems have provided community directories, organised projects dealing with older people, childcare problems, facilities and jobs for young people, and establishing community newspapers.

The 'patch' system is geographically based. The district team, or part of it, is located in a particular section of a community and is responsible for dealing with all the problems arising in that neighbourhood (Rosenthal, 1983). The task of 'patch' social workers in this situation is to get to know the community – its problems and its resources, both formal and informal. Social workers eventually become acquainted with nearly all the residents in their small area, their informal networks, and the organisations operating within it, including those of a voluntary and statutory nature. The converse is also true: the community gets to know the social workers. Through time, the social workers become easily recognisable and more accessible to the community. One of the aims of the 'patch' system is to reduce the dichotomy between the 'expert' professional and the 'dependent' client. This is usually attempted by fostering self-help groups which either already exist or are started by social workers. Self-help groups can become dependent on social workers if they act as initiators of the action and gatekeepers of resources (Davis, 1982). Furthermore, the social worker acts in the capacity of 'patch' leader whilst the locally recruited volunteers are placed in subordinate roles as 'patch' workers. Organising the system in this way reinforces residents' dependent status in backing up professionals. Placing the community's activities in a subordinate role devalues its contribution. The diminution of community involvement through hierarchy, is additional to that provided by the exploitation of its labour on either an unpaid voluntary or low-paid basis. Home-helps, street wardens and other ancillary and domestic workers are the backbone of the 'patch' system, yet, they constitute the bulk of its low paid echelons. They are also primarily women. Besides using volunteers as 'patch' workers, the 'patch' system draws other lay members of the community, professionals and councillors into its ranks.

The 'patch' leader must ensure close liaison and consultation between local participants and the members of the social services team, and aim to use both community and departmental resources in the most effective manner when meeting identified needs. The priorities guiding the 'patch' leader in the allocation of resources are those of utilising the informal support networks, self-help groups, and voluntary groups first, and the resources of the statutory services last. This policy has meant that the rationing of social services can continue unnoticed as long as community resources procured by the state on either a free or cheap basis are used to replace them.

Some 'patch' systems have attempted to reduce the powers of the professional workers through a Social Care Assembly (SCA) in which community participants are drawn into the decision-making processes. However, since the SCA is usually formulated on the basis of its being non-sectarian and non-political, it can mystify the power relations permeating the 'patch' system. By involving local residents in decision-making on day-to-day matters, the political realities determining the overall allocation of resources are ignored. Such involvement gives people a false sense of power in which determination of the part is taken to subsume determination of the whole. The mystification of these power relations is conducive to the retention of the *status quo* and should be recognised as the political stance which it is. Furthermore, the ultimate veto of the professional social worker in matters encompassed by the day-to-day decision-making process is masked. The SCA exists because the social workers have decided that it will and the consultation process occurs because they are willing to listen. Consultation falls far short of holding full and equal power.

A measure of worker equality amongst social workers operating a 'patch' system takes place by assigning a number of tasks to each worker and expecting a worker to know all aspects of the work. However, status inequality can occur through the recognition of certain specialisms over others. Additionally, earlier professional differentiation is perpetuated through the remuneration system which remains based on the workers' previous classification (Cooper, 1980). Also, the 'patch' system does not have a career structure. This penalises 'patch' employees in the social services department's internal promotion stakes. 'Patch' workers may have to leave to acquire promotion elsewhere.

Women are central to the 'patch' system as both paid and unpaid workers. Many of the support services and voluntary tasks are performed by women. The work alloted to them has increased in complexity and changed from being simply about physical caring to providing advice and making preliminary assessments of needs. If paid, their wages do not reflect the level of responsibility they hold. These changes in the labour process at the lower levels of the social services hierarchy reflect the system's concern with making maximum use of resources, even if it means exploiting women's labour and interest in the well-being of others. Meanwhile, the posts at the upper reaches of the social work profession are held primarily by men (Coyle and Skinner, 1988). Outside of the 'patch' system, women are expected to provide support at the informal, unpaid level by both keeping an eye on their neighbours and looking after their kin. Women's commitment to seeing people receive the care they need is more than taken for granted. They are expected to provide the care required, without formal external backing. Women pay a price for being overburdened with caring work (Burden and Gottlieb, 1987). It takes the form of mental illness, relying on tranquillisers to see them through the day, and simple frustration at being at everyone's beck and call (Ashurst and Hall, 1989). Institutional racism and the lack of resources meeting black people's needs intensifies the caring burden borne by black women and increases the pressures operating against their well-being (Malek, 1985).

The 'patch' system does engage the community to a certain extent, but its involvement falls far short of the principle aim of community action, that of redistributing power and resources in favour of the powerless. For this to occur, the community must become a real partner in the 'patch' system with the power to determine key overall decisions affecting policy formulation and the allocation of resources as well as day-to-day ones. To overcome some of the disparities between workers, a career structure must be incorporated into the 'patch' system. More importantly, hierarchical differentiation and its role in involving community participants in a subordinate position needs to be questioned. 'Patch' systems have not directly addressed either gender or 'race' based inequality.

Feminist community workers holding positions in 'patch' systems can identify inequalities stemming from social divisions and play a role in initiating organisational change geared to meeting the interests of women workers and consumers more effectively. They can also work to develop feminist services, networks and support groups amongst women in the community. Additionally, they can establish groups to monitor the impact of the 'patch' system on services in the community.

Power Sharing in Hierarchical Institutions

Consumer participation and the more direct involvement of basic grade social workers in the decision-making processes within the social services department is of interest to social workers keen to democratise their services and management aiming to reduce costs. Social workers feel that their day-to-day knowledge of client needs and responses are particularly relevant in determining policy issues but lack the institutional mechanisms for drawing their understanding into policy formulation. Many social workers resent their powerlessness and inability to influence decisions. Yet, they are often responsible for implementing policies which are developed without consulting them and with which they may totally disagree. Users are also excluded from policy making once they have cast their vote and elected a particular political party to power. The 'patch' system at least offers social workers and users an opportunity to effect policy formulation and service delivery.

Middle level management instructed to respond to political directives emanating from central government which has not sought its advice also feels increasingly disempowered. Caught between the pressures of grassroots consumers and workers pushing for increased and better services on the one hand, and those of their political masters demanding cuts in services on the other, middle management finds itself in an extremely contradictory and powerless position. The untenable nature of middle management's position opens the possibility of an alliance to improve service delivery involving middle managers, fieldworkers and consumers (Dominelli and Leonard, 1982). Power sharing alliances also pose the question of the extent to which consumers can be involved in decision-making processes to promote their own welfare in institutions which remain as hierarchical as social services departments.

Democratising decision-making within hierarchical institutions is a difficult process. It involves making alliances with a number of individuals and groups both within the organisation and outside it. This includes trade unionists, the women's movement, black activists, academic consultants sympathetic to these aims and objectives. If formed into a supportive network, these groups can provide leverage in promoting this cause, offering advice, theoretical direction, and practical help.

Social workers embarking on the process of democratising their workplace can damage their promotion prospects, become subject to disciplinary procedures, or get dismissed. Those that have become involved in such processes have found taking protective measures before forming alliances with management a wise precation (see Dominelli and Leonard, 1982). Such moves have included safeguarding the interests of clients by having the social services department provide cover for the work that is normally done with them, thereby freeing workers to engage in developing links with the community and management; having time spent on developing these links acknowledged as part of workers' normal workload; and ensuring that social workers' democratising efforts do not facilitate 'cuts' in services or become incorporated as meaningless parts serving the *status quo*. Moreover, taking steps to reduce the powers of superiors to institutionalise adverse judgements of workers whose political views they dislike has also been necessary. Establishing some form of parity between social workers and management has required that the following principles be upheld:

* equality between participants;
* democratic decision-making;
* confidentiality of proceedings within the group;
* mutual accountability;
* developing power bases within the department and in the community; and
* Collective action.

Adherence to these principles is essential if the momentum of collaborative work is to continue over time and counter the forces endorsing differentiation and suspicion between the different groups involved in power sharing endeavours (Dominelli and Leonard, 1982).

To facilitate their work, participants have found it useful to clarify the organisational features they are aiming to change, and share these as their unifying goals; obtain the factual information they require; know the institutions they seek to change, the people with which they are dealing, and the resources they have available. They should be familiar with the power structure, the political alignments of the people involved in it, and understand the organisations which they are trying to influence. Most of this information is readily available, but people may have difficulty bringing it together and using it to affect organisational processes, other professionals, and the community.

Social workers and middle management attempting to push back the boundaries of hierarchical decision-making structures have had to develop their own support groups to help them promote their democratisation process and implement the strategy and tactics entailed in doing so. This has also involved forming alliances outside of the social services department and encompassed clients, tenants, trade unions and various community groups. When embarking on social change of this nature, women have found it essential to form autonomous women-only support groups to identify their particular needs and interests, develop confidence in their own abilities and ideas, and establish networking groups (Hanmer and Statham, 1989; Stanley and Wise, 1983; Dreifus, 1973; Hooks, 1984; Boston Women's Health Collective, 1979). Black people have also found it necessary to develop autonomous support groups to enhance their abilities and promote their interests (Rooney, 1987; Hooks, 1984; Malek, 1985; Lorde, 1984). Community groups involved in the process of democratising hierarchical institutions have also developed support networks. Their formation has been important in ensuring the collective strength of community groups and providing community based social workers with community backing. Community groups have created their support groups whilst simultaneously organising to put forward their own demands and monitoring the services the social services department is already placing at their disposal (see Rooney, 1987).

Once embarked on the process of altering decision-making within their employing agencies, participants have confronted a mixture of advances and reverses in the realisation of their project. Being prepared for such patchy results makes it easier for those involved to cope with them. They also need to face the possibility of total failure and dismissal from their posts. Support groups can facilitate the process of grieving over frustrated ambitions and learning from the experience. Collective action can take time to develop and, in the interim period, as women have found out, it is important to retain a sense of humour, radical perspective and patience.

35

Chapter 2
Feminist Campaigns and Networks

Feminists have been extensively involved in social action aiming to restore women's human, political, economic and social rights. Feminist campaigns and networks have been crucial vehicles for furthering these objectives and have produced some of the most innovative community work in Britain. Feminist campaigns and networks take women's gender based oppression as their starting point, set about eradicating it by changing social relations in their very practice and, make it form the basis of feminist community work. Important feminist campaigns challenging the existing configuration of social relations have included abortion issues (Greenwood and Young, 1976) – The National Abortion Campaign (NAC); reproductive rights (Frankfort, 1972; Davis, *et al*, 1988) – The Reproductive Rights Campaign (RRC); decriminialising prostitution (McLeod, 1982) – The Programme for the Reform of the Law on Soliciting (PROS); providing women with refuges (Binney *et al*, 1981; Scottish Women's Aid Federation, 1980; Wilson, 1983) – The National Women's Aid Federation (NWAF) campaigns; and securing better health facilities for women (Doyal, 1983; Ruzek, 1978 and 1986) – women's health collectives established throughout the country. Feminist campaigns have introduced new features to community action. Foremost amongst these have been the development of a new sense of solidarity and strength amongst women; extending the subjects covered by community action and developing new forms of community organisation (Adamson *et al.*, 1988). Women involved in feminist campaigns have provided demonstrable evidence that women can organise themselves effectively to improve conditions regarding specific issues, (e.g. prostitution) or to defend hard-earned gains, (e.g. abortion). Through their actions, the myth of female passivity has received a hard knock.

Many women have acquired the confidence and skills they need to challenge definitions of their reality and confront even the most powerful with these. For instance, PROS women have mounted a publicity campaign in which the hardened police chiefs' definition of prostitution has been effectively debunked. Though this definition is by no means accepted by all, PROS has succeeded in providing an alternative view of prostitution – that it is a job with validity and social usefulness (McLeod, 1982). The redefinition of women's problems has been a major development of feminist campaigns.

Through the redefinition of social issues, feminists have also been able to place at the top of the agenda, men's role in creating problems for women and children. For instance, the NWAF campaign against marital violence has demonstrated that the acceptability of social attitudes condoning the male prerogative of disciplining women through physcial and emotional abuse legitimised male violence in domestic situations. Furthermore, NWAF has revealed that women have been unable to leave violent partners not because they are mentally defective, as some suggest, but because the material conditions necessary for them to do so, for example, jobs, housing and money, simply have not been available to them.

Women Against Violence Against Women (WAVAW) in their more general attack on male violence, which ranges from pornography to rape, have forced people to consider male aggression in a new light (Lederer, 1982; McNeil and Rhodes, 1985). WAVAW have argued that since males are the aggressors men, and not their female victims, should be punished. For example, WAVAW called for a male curfew during the days when the Yorkshire Ripper stalked women on the streets of Leeds. The demonstrations of women involved in Women Reclaim the Night have reinforced this message. However, their approach has ignored the impact of racism and required specific action to counter it (Hooks, 1984; Bryan *et al*, 1985).

Another important feature of feminist campaigns has been their success in achieving a broad base of support for their activities by calling on trade unions and professional organisations to endorse their demands. Activating such support has required women to organise within these organisations over a period of time. These activities have formed part of feminists' commitment to raising consciousness. Their efforts locally have ultimately coalesced in securing trade union support for their struggles nationally at the level of the Trade Union Congress (TUC) for example, the homeworkers' campaign (Hopkins, 1982), and reproductive rights campaign. Feminists have succeeded in getting many male trade unionists, particularly those in public sector unions where female membership is high, to acknowledge that lack of control over their fertility has affected women's employment and that it is necessary for women to have this control if equal opportunity in the workplace is to underpin their working lives and career prospects. In this manner, feminists have redefined issues previously ranked 'private' as social ones.

There have been other forces endorsing feminists' demands, for example, state concern over the extreme overcrowding in British prisons has contributed towards the acceptability of the broader decriminalisation campaign; public concern over the rights of children and their welfare has affected people's views on domestic violence. Women's interests have come to the fore, primarily because feminists have organised to ensure this happens. Furthermore, feminist social action promoting women's welfare has demonstrated that children's and men's welfare is badly served by current social arrangements. For example, marital violence has been exposed as damaging children's, men's and women's emotional existence. Feminists' work on this score has highlighted the urgency of challenging the male stereotype and providing men with the help and support networks necessary for them to break the confines of their oppressing and oppressive roles (Dominelli, 1982).

Feminist campaigns, aimed at securing social justice for women, have implications for all those abhoring injustice, wherever it occurs. This moral rightness has been another decisive factor in providing women's campaigns with support and sympathy from individuals and organisations which are not predominantly feminist in their orientation. Through such supporters, further opportunities for feminists to secure resources for their campaigns have become available. These in turn have become part of the campaign's broader support networks which now cover feminist as well as non-feminist groups. The broad ranging nature of such support networks enhances the possibility that the social changes engendered by these campaigns encompass more than women's concerns. But expanding their support networks has also held back the feminist challenge and instead of transforming social relations, their campaigns have resulted in piecemeal reforms which have left the *status quo* intact. For example, American feminists have found that changing the legislation on abortion has ended up working against the interests of women when doctors discovered there were enormous profits to be made by providing abortions to women who wanted them (Frankfort, 1972). Abortion clinics have turned abortion into a commodity and initiated a process of medical treatment which has left women feeling powerless and exploited (Worcester and Whatley, 1988).

Nonetheless, some feminist changes have permeated hierarchical institutions such as the social services department, residential homes and the probation service and challenged them organisationally and practically (see McLeod, 1982). The NWAF's work on domestic violence has exposed the social services department's relative neglect and lack of understanding of the needs of women suffering from domestic violence and forced many social services departments to provide resources, including refuges, for abused women. The NWAF's stance on women's self-determination and

democratic decision-making for the women living in their refuges
has promoted the adoption of such practices in some local
authority refuges. This contrasts with the authoritarian way in
which most local authority residential homes are run and organised. NWAF refuges have demonstrated that women, stigmatised
as clients, can run their own lives if given the opportunity and
the resources required for doing so (Binney *et al*, 1983).

Social workers and probation officers who have become involved
in feminist campaigns have found it necessary to develop internal
support groups. This has involved creating support networks
amongst colleagues and sympathetic managerial staff within their
employing authority. Such support has been essential, not only for
the furtherance of their campaign's objectives, but to ease the
sense of isolation and despair workers have often felt when facing
their organisation's intransigence and resistance to demands for
change (McLeod, 1982).

This chapter will consider feminist campaigns and networks in
terms of the processes through which feminist community workers
identify problems that need to be addressed, the ways in which
women organise collectively and the difficulties they have to
resolve in successfully involving women in collective action in the
community. We will examine feminist campaigns around childcare,
violence to women and children in the home, child sexual abuse,
and peace. We highlight how feminist community action uses 'the
personal is political' as its central organising principle to redefine
matters which society relegates to the private realm (and therefore
outside the scope for intervention) as social issues which affect
everyone. Consideration is also given to how women identify the
techniques and skills required for redefining problems in feminist
directions and work for their resolution in accordance with feminist principles. This includes examining feminist attempts to introduce non-hierarchical ways of working into their activities,
develop their own support networks and use their experience as
women to relate to other women. In addition, we consider
concerns that women share regardless of their status in the labour
market.

Characteristics of Feminist Campaigns and Networks

Feminist campaigns and networks have featured significantly in
the feminist political landscape and have played a key role in
establishing feminist community work. As major forms of feminist
collective organisation, feminist campaigns and networks have been
used to promote feminist understandings of social issues and
eliminate gender oppression. Feminist campaigns and networks are
fluid entities structured around a group or groups of women
working to change a particular aspect of their reality as part of
the process of eradicating sexist oppression. Feminist campaigns

are normally issue based and may involve direct action, including demonstrations and mass movements on a national or even international level, for example, the Women's Peace Movement (Cook and Kirk, 1983), or they may be small localised affairs in which a group of women offer each other support and seek specific resources for their cause, for example, Southwark Asian Women's Aid (Malek, 1985). Feminist networks can also be *ad hoc* support groups. At times, the distinction between a campaign and a network may be blurred. For example, the National Women's Aid Federation is a campaigning organisation which has a national network of refuges women can draw on. Feminist campaigns and networks form part of the process of feminist activity in transforming social relations which begins with a redefinition of social problems.

Redefining social problems from a feminist perspective is crucial to challenging prevailing definitions of issues and developing feminist consciousness. It is also a preliminary step in the formation of feminist campaigns and networks. Redefining social problems from a feminist perspective demystifies social relations and reveals the extent to which these subordinate women and work to their detriment. Some of the earliest feminist campaigns and networks have been developed by radical feminists tackling male violence, particularly men's domestic physical violence against and rape of women. This has entailed redefining the issue from a personal problem between men and women, to a social matter involving all men and women because such behaviour has been legitimised by the subordinate position women hold in society (Brownmiller, 1976). Since then, other forms of male violence such as pornography and the global nuclear threat have been addressed. Feminist analyses have demonstrated how the pattern of male violence, which begins with men showing contempt for women by calling them derogatory names such as 'bitch', 'broad' and 'whore' and denying them their human rights and dignity and ends in a deep-seated hatred of women legitimising rape or taking their lives. At the time of writing (6 December 1989) a man walked into the University of Montreal and committed femicide. Fourteen women engineering students were gunned down in the classroom by a man, claiming to hate feminists, because these women had dared enter men's world by becoming engineers. He was making the point that women's place in the community is not in the public world of waged work but in the privacy of the home, ministering to the needs of men. It is precisely these definitions of women's position and their role in society that feminists seek to challenge.

In redefining society's understanding of male violence against women, feminists have focused on the social construction of masculinity and femininity rather than on biological attributes and have highlighted the significance of the following points (Brown-miller, 1976; Lederer, 1982; Gordon, 1986):

* *Gender.* Men violate women's rights to a safe environment by assaulting them;
* *Gender neutral language.* The use of gender neutral language masks gender power relations by obscuring the fact that men are the attackers and women their victims;
* *Power.* Men's sexual attacks on women are about power, not about sex, or men's biological urges;
* *Normality.* Men who attack women are 'normal', not psycho-paths;
* *Control.* In sanctioning men's right to control women, society legitimates men's use of violence against and abuse of women;
* *Mysogeny.* Personal sexism is rooted in individual men's hatred of and contempt for women;
* *Institutional sexism.* Society's treatment of women victims of men's physical and sexual aggression reinforces the abuse of women. The police, judiciary, courts and public hold women responsible for the attack;
* *Subordination of women.* Women's subordinate social position endorses men's belief in their right to force women to comply with their wishes;
* *Women's strength.* Women's strength has enabled them to survive their harrowing ordeals and move out of the passive victim role; and
* *Women's voice.* Feminist theory and practice is based on women's own accounts of their experiences, thereby giving ordinary women a voice rather than conceding expertise on their condition to professionals.

Unearthing the dynamics of male violence, bringing these into public consciousness, and strengthening the capacities of women who have been attacked to survive, form the basis of feminist campaigns and networks on these issues. For example, American feminists in the anti-rape movement organised a Rape Speak-Out in New York in 1971. This provided women with a forum in which to break the isolation and fear that had prevented them from placing their ordeals in the public arena and begin the process of educating Americans about the realities of rape (Davis, 1989). Feminsits in Berkeley set-up a community based 24-hour crisis line known as the Bay Area Women Against Rape in that same year. This became the crisis centre which has provided the model for the rape crisis centres created by feminists in the rest of America and other countries (Davis, 1989). The purpose of these centres was for women to support women struggling to transcend the pain and disability engendered by the assault on their person and sustain women feeling able to do so, report the crime and proceed with a court case.

Since those early days, feminists have also uncovered the extent of sexual assaults against female children, particularly within the alleged sanctity of the family. They have developed a network of Incest Survivor Groups to support their healing process (Kelly, 1988; Dominelli, 1986 and 1989; Armstrong, 1988). Feminist social action on sexual violence has also revealed that young boys are also physically and sexually abused by adult men. They have also highlighted the problematic nature of the dominant ideology of masculinity (McLeod, 1982), and the pressures society places on men to conform to the unfeeling, aggressive, macho stereotypical man (see Festau, 1975; Tolson, 1977; Bowl, 1985). Anti-sexist men have begun to take up some of the issues feminist insights have exposed. So although feminism begins the process of eliminating sexist oppression by focusing on women's issues, its work uncovers the stunted emotional development of children and men and promotes action aimed at ensuring their well-being. Eliminating sexism will enhance the quality of life for children, women and men (Dominelli and McLeod, 1989).

Redefining Social Problems

A key understanding of the feminist movement is that relationships between individuals are imbued with power relations rooted in the ideology of female subordination and male supremacy. This has given rise to the often quoted phrase the 'personal is political' as a shorthand standing for the complex ways in which sexual politics pervade every aspect of women's lives, from the most intimate to the most removed (Millett, 1969). Sexual polilitics are about power – the socially legitimised power of men to control women and the unacknowledged power of women to resist that control and assert their right to live according to egalitarian principles, which do not presuppose the subjugation of others. Feminists have reached this understanding collectively by examining their individual experiences as women and comparing these with those of other women in similar situations. Such insights initially arose in fairly loose, unstructured meetings between women who came together to make sense of their positions. Meetings of this nature were to become more widespread and address women's issues more systematically. These get-togethers have provided the basis of consciousness-raising groups (Dreifus, 1973), which now feature strongly in the feminist organisational repertoire.

Consciousness-raising groups have enabled women to draw on their personal experience in understanding both their oppression and that of other women and seeking its social causation (Morgan, 1971). In the early days of the women's liberation movement, women, particularly white middle class women concluded, from their own experiences in consciousness-raising groups, that women's oppression featured universally in women's lives (Hooks, 1984). Neglecting other dimensions through which oppression occurs, they subsumed the experience of all women under their own (see Freidan, 1963). Lesbian women, working class women and black women have rejected this analysis (see Lorde, 1984; Hooks, 198 ; Davis, 1984; Carby, 1982; Amos and Parmar, 1984; Wilson, 1986) and highlighted how differences arising from women's sexual orientation, class, 'race', age and physical and mental impairment have made women's experience of oppression complex and varied. From this it follows that sisterhood is something that has to be worked for rather than just assumed. Nonetheless, women's experience of oppression as women has been crucial in redefining social problems in ways that has revealed the gendered impact of social relations (Morgan, 1971).

Feminist community workers have been able to draw on women's personal experience of oppression when identifying issues that have needed to be addressed through women's collective action. By bringing women together in groups, feminist community workers have worked with women to redefine social problems and challenge the individualising and pathologising approaches to women's issues marking the practice of traditional community workers and social workers. Crucial to this challenge has been undoing the division of social problems into private matters requiring individual or family solutions and public issues in which a range of social forces including the state, formal agencies and the public intervened.

Organising collectively has also given women the courage to speak out, making their voices heard and their suffering known. Violence to women in the home exemplifies a key phenomenon which was treated as a private matter until feminist campaigns, of the early 1970s, revealed that the definition of domestic violence as a private issue legitimised its occurrence, blamed women who were caught within its web, and left women who wished to escape it without access to the resources necessary for this to happen (Scottish Women's Aid Federation, 1980). Feminist campaigns have made domestic violence a social issue and established a network of refuges to support women leaving violent partners. Moreover, feminist analyses of domestic violence have revealed how society's definitions of masculinity and femininity is based on women's subordinate postion and has underwritten the acceptability of men using force to control women, thereby making every member of society responsible both for the perpetuation of domestic violence and its elimination.

Childcare has been another arena in which feminists have questioned the view that it is a private task to be undertaken by women in the home. This is not to argue that feminists are demanding that the state becomes an instrument for the surveillance family life, but that society acknowledges children as a social responsibility with rights of their own rather than puppets parents dangle on a string. This means that social resources are necessary to provide unstigmatised and stimulating childcare for all children and that childcare cease being the sole responsibility of women (David and New, 1985). The National Childcare Campaign (NCC), though unsuccessful so far, has aimed to secure publicly funded child-centered childcare in Britain. The NCC has also enabled women to make connections between their low status in the home and their low pay in the workforce (NCC, 1985). Employers assume women will work for only short periods before leaving the workforce to start a family, and therefore deny them access to training, more prestigious work or updating their skills (Armstrong, 1984; Aldred, 1981).

There are dangers in redefining social problems without taking account of other social divisions which feminists have not always successfully avoided. These may reinforce other forms of oppression and undermine feminists' struggle to eradicate gender inequality. For example, ignoring the interconnectedness of racism and sexism in matters of sexual violence has meant that early white radical feminist demands, in both Britain and America, inadvertently confirmed racist views of black men as the main assailants (Bryan *et al*, 1985; Hooks, 1984; Davis, 1989). Black feminists have pointed out that without including racism in their analysis white feminists actions on rape fed racist myths of black men's criminality and sexual appetites and disregarded facts – most rapes are committed by white men, and white men are more likely to rape black women than black men rape white women (Davis, 1989). White feminists are now responding to this critique and becoming more sensitive to the interaction between racism and sexism (Barrett and McIntosh, 1985). Black feminists' challenge has facilitated the development of white feminist principles of listening to other women's accounts of their experience and using these to develop less oppressive forms of social action. This approach means that feminist action is always in the process of adapting to new insights and understandings, thereby lending an open and unfinished character to it.

Organising Tips

Problem Definition
1) Who defines the problem?
2) For whom is it a problem?
3) What is the problem?

Identifying which Problems Feminists Address

The issues women seek to address in transforming private woes into social concerns are related to their experience of gender oppression. There are no areas of life, private or public, outside the feminists' remit. So far, feminists have tackled issues ranging from physical and sexual assaults against women in the home to the militarisation of the world (Davis, 1989). In redefining social problems, feminists have focused on women's resistance to oppression in countless ways, some public, some private, some effective, some ineffective and the internalisation of gender oppression which blocks women's progress in divesting themselves of it. Feminists have shown how women actively create history. Women are neither passive victims in a historic process nor robots dancing to men's tunes. Feminists have also described the role material circumstances play in contributing to women's oppression and preventing them from becoming free of it. For example, battered women remain with violent partners because they realise that without adequate housing and an income of their own, they are vulnerable outside this relationship as well as within it. But even within violent relationships, women actively take steps to minimise the violence perpetrated against them by their male partners. Trying not to annoy him or overtly challenge his views are all part of a strategy aimed at securing their safety.

Feminists have drawn on bringing women together in groups to discuss issues and raise their consciousness about them. By sharing their personal experiences, women have been able to identify common problems (Dreifus, 1973). Seeing that they were experiencing similar problems in somewhat different circumstances has enabled women in these groups to challenge the view that they have precipitated these by their (in)action and inadequacies and realise that their predicament has a social basis. Continued discussion aimed at understanding their situation and developing strategies for changing it have given these groups a crucial role in fostering women's confidence and self-esteem (Curno *et al*, 1982). These in turn have empowered women and enabled them to speak out publicly with their stories and experiences, challenging accepted definitions of their problems and stereotypes about the passivity of women in the process (South Wales Association of Tenants, 1982).

The women's movement has consisted of a number of diverse initiatives ranging from a woman writing from her own experience through a couple of women getting together to talk about their lives to larger groups organising mass campaigns around community issues. This has given the feminist movement a rich variety of organisational forms, although it may have increased its fragmented appearance. Whilst its fragmentation may be a weakness in certain situations, for example – organising women nationally and internationally (Wilson, 1986) – it is a strength in others, for example – giving women the space to pursue their interests in the most appropriate way for them (Segal, 1987). Eschewing dogma is a central tenet of feminist theory and action. Having women develop the form of organisation best suited to their purposes facilitates holding to this principle in practice. Whilst some issues have readily attracted support from a cross-section of women (for example, the issues raised by the Working Women's Charter – Wilson, 1986; Segal, 1987) others have required more sustained action in becoming popularly recognised (for example, women's right to express their sexuality with other women (Hunt, 1990). Some issues have been initially addressed by a small group of women who have relied on other women to subsequently join and support their efforts in achieving widespread support for them. As in the case of the feminist social workers tackling child sexual abuse who had to overcome a credibility gap in which their analysis has been vehemently rejected (see Bell, 1988).

The feminist movement has been castigated for presenting itself as the property of white middle class feminists (Hooks, 1984; Bryan et al., 1985). But an examination of the struggles women have undertaken in the community reveals that feminist activities have been undertaken by a range of women – working-class women, middle-class women, black women, white women, older women, disabled women and lesbians. The issues which each group has chosen to highlight and devote its energies have been different; and their definition of the problem and approach to it have alienated certain other groups of women (see Wilson, 1986). For example, the white feminists' call for 'abortion on demand' alienated black women who pointed out that their problem was that abortions and sterilisations were forced upon them (Hooks, 1984; Bryan et al, 1985). This led to a more acceptable redefinition of the problem as a woman's right to control her fertility in the manner most appropriate for her and the campaigns against sterilisation abuse (Sidel, 1986). This propensity of feminist action tackling one problem to uncover others is a feature of the movement (Dominelli and McLeod, 1989).

Feminists also need to beware of minimising or not recognising the struggles of women lacking access to the media and publishers (see Hunt, 1990). Acknowledging this pitfall is vital if working class and black women's struggles are not to be devalued and made invisible. It is very easy, in the era of mass communications, for women keyed into communication networks to define the terrain of the women's movement, simply because in the eyes of the media, their concerns make better copy. But women without access to such resources are also struggling to improve the conditions of their lives. Their efforts may be unsung, but they exist nonetheless.

Examples of this are working class and black feminist struggles to survive by securing decent housing, childcare provisions and equality at work. Working class and black feminists have used trade unions and other workplace based organisations to gain rights in waged employment, whilst simultaneously challenging the racist and sexist nature of these organisations. Moreover, they have had to make the connections between their position in the workforce and the community during these struggles. For example, black women's struggling at Mansfield Hosiery and Grunwick were able to draw heavily on community support networks which they had nurtured over the years to sustain them in their protracted battles with recalcitrant employers. At the same time, they had to use community pressure to shift the trade union movement from its sexist and racist positions. In the strike at Mansfield Hosiery, the trade union concerned was a major obstacle to black women achieving equality in the workplace (CIR, 1973). At Grunwick, the trade union movement adopted a more enlightened position, but failed to support women in ways endorsing anti-sexist and anti-racist practice.

Women Getting in Touch with Other Women by Organising

Women have relied on networking to form contact with other women. Networking may be very informal. It may mean women simply asking other women they know to join them in examining an issue and helping them make sense of it (Curno *et al*, 1982). These women then ask other women to come along and so a group is formed. This adds a personal dimension to networking, making women feel more comfortable when discussing issues than if facing a group of strangers. Establishing a trusting and relaxed atmosphere in which women feel free to be frank is essential in sharing their experiences. Other more formal approaches include women putting up notices of a meeting in places frequented by women, for example, laundrettes, washrooms, doctors' surgeries. Women may print leaflets calling other women to join their group in a particular activity. Or, they may use community newspapers to run feature articles on their work and invite women to join them. Their oppression as women links group members together and enables them to empathise with other women's plight when they may not have undergone that particular experience of it (Dreifus, 1973). However, empathising may fall short of truly understanding specific instances of oppression and feminists desist from speaking on behalf of other women.

Women's participation in these meetings is squeezed between their domestic commitments and their waged work. Many women have to surmount considerable hostility from male partners who resent their taking an interest in feminist activities, and may require support in handling the conflict which arises in their intimate relationships (South Wales Association of Tenants, 1982). Women run considerable personal risks when participating in feminist campaigns. The following account explains the fears of a woman involved in the occupation of Afan Council Offices:

> 'Ceri started to cry. She said she didn't want to go home but she'd got to. She hadn't told her husband she was going on the sit-in. She'd just told him she was going to a meeting. She said that she hadn't dared tell him she was going to stay out all night (let alone three nights!) because he would have stopped her going. Now, she thought, he bound to beat her up.' (South Wales Association of Tenants, 1982:25).

Although Ceri's husband surprised her by admiring her stance because she had appeared on TV, the episode forced this women's group to re-appraise its work, tactics and achievements and consider the link between personal relations and political activity. This highlighted the significance of integrating theory and practice and learning from personal experience.

Feminist groups take account of women's domestic responsibilities in the provision of childminding facilities and the timing of meetings. Making connections between the different spheres within which women operate is essential if more women are to be drawn into feminist campaigns and networks. Having services which ease women's participation in feminist activities is in keeping with the feminist principle that 'the personal is political'. Reducing power differentials between women and making it possible for more women to attend and make their contribution to the group's business are other important dimensions of this. However, reducing power differentials between women goes beyond this. Egalitarianism has to permeate relationships within the group. Feminists have tried reducing the power that stems from people having formal positions within groups by eliminating positions of power, or by sharing them, so that all women gain the skills of the job and no one holds a post long enough to form a clique bolstering individual power (Tyneside Rape Crisis Centre Collective, 1982). Additionally, women share the power that is derived from expertise by sharing their knowledge with each other.

These dynamics have structured feminist campaigns and networks, featuring strongly, for example, in the women's health movement. Women share medical knowledge and attempt to reduce the hierarchy that comes from the doctors controlling medical knowledge which, if accessible to patients, would facilitate their taking a more active role in their treatment (Ruzek, 1978; Foster, 1989; Doyal, 1983). Reducing inegalitarian relationships within groups is not easy (Barker, 1986). Despite brave attempts to counter hierarchical relationships, these can creep into feminist organisations. Working class women have complained that group processes organised by middle class women favour the more articulate who are familier with expressing themselves verbally (Finch, 1983; Davis, 1988). Moreover, middle class women have access to resources that promote participation in group activities (Torkington, 1981). These are denied working class women and can engender hierarchy by excluding women who cannot purchase them. It is evident that a hierarchy exists which gives middle class women a voice whilst denying working class and black women theirs. An example of this is seen in feminist academic conferences which charge high fees thus preventing women from lower income groups from joining them. The Fourth International Congress on Women, scheduled at Hunter College in New York, is charging between \$US200 and \$US275 in conference fees alone. On the local level, middle class feminists have subsidised working class women's participation in groups by providing transportation, paying for telephone calls, stationery etc., (Torkington, 1981).

Feminist groups have also organised around political decisions affecting women's everyday lives. For example, social security regulations such as the British 'cohabitation rule' and the American 'man about the house rule' assume women's financial dependency on men (Land, 1976; Sidel, 1986). In England, Special Claims Squads (SCS) have attempted to force single parent women having any contact with men to become financially dependent on them. Their activities have intimidated women into dropping social security claims. They have also prompted feminists to organise women to protect themselves. The Women's Right to Income Group challenged the activities of SCS by redefining the problem as one of ensuring women's right to an independent income (Torkington, 1981). Their activities have revealed that whilst the personal is political, the political is also personal.

Campaigning Aids, Techniques and Tips

Campaigning requires specific organisational skills to mobilise people and generate support for a cause, gather the information necessary to identify an issue and present it to others, procure the material and human resources necessary for mounting a campaign and ensure that action remains under the direction of the campaigning group. Effectively implementing these tasks involves organisational, political, communicative and interpersonal know-how. In organising terms, feminists working with women in the community have sought to keep hold of principles upholding social justice, equality, women's control over their lives and democratic decision-making in their practice. These concerns have concentrated feminists' energies on sharing skills and knowledge with other women, acquiring and retaining control of their organisations, building women's confidence, reducing conflict between

49

workers in and users of facilities and developing strategies which focus on finding consensual 'win-win' solutions to problems (Brandwein, 1987). Besides redefining social problems, feminist campaigns and networks have brought the *processes* whereby issues are tackled and the relationships which community workers establish with community groups, centre stage. Whilst some of these, e.g. intragroup dynamics and consciousness-raising techniques, are covered in the following chapters, this section draws on the principles, techniques and skills feminists have used in their campaigning activities to provide organising tips useful to social workers and community workers of both genders adopting practices consistent with feminist organisational principles in reaching out to their constituents.

Forming Support Groups and Alliances to Realise your Strategy

* What kind of support does your group need?
* What groups/individuals can it call upon?
* At what point does your group ask for external support?
* How long does your group require this support?

Resources Required in Implementing an Action Plan

* What resources do you require:
  – personnel;
  – material; and
  – organisational?
* Where can you obtain these resources:
  – group;
  – supporters;
  – public agencies;
  – commercial bodies; and
  – others.
* How much money is required to obtain these resources?
* For what period of time are these resources required?

Running Facilities for Women

* What are the aims of the facility?
  – What do community workers hope to achieve?
  – What do users want to achieve?
    Consider building confidence and self-esteem.
    Consider fostering independence in women and enabling them to stand up for their rights.
    Consider developing services that will meet the needs of different groups of women, e.g., black women, lesbian women, older women, disabled women.

- What does the group hope to achieve in terms of the public? Consider consciousness-raising and political education.
★ Who will make the decisions and how?
  - Distinguish between collective decisions and individual ones.
  - Develop ways of combatting hierarchy and promoting equality.
  - Endorse democratic decision-making.
  - Adoption of policies which do not discriminate against other women, for example, black women, older women, disabled women, lesbian women.
★ Keeping records of the facility's activities, funds, expenditures.
★ What facilities will be available to women?
★ Who will have access to the facility?
  - Access by users, workers and those they invite.
  - Protection for users and workers, especially important if the facility is a refuge.
  - Ensure that the facility is accessible to women with disabilities, that it meets fire, building, and health and safety regulations.
★ Who will be the users of the facility?
  - How will they find out about the facility?
  - Will they be able to self-refer or be referred by others?
  - How will they be involved in running the facility?
★ - What skills sharing, formal advice services, professional services, and educative functions will the facility offer users?
  - What support services will the facility offer women? Consider childminding provsions, recreational services, meeting rooms, privacy within the facility.
  - Consider training facilities, housing, employment and other needs women may need access to outside of the facility.
★ How will the facility be funded, maintained and repaired?
★ What attitudes and policies will the facility adopt towards male visitors?
  - For example, excluding violent partners from refuges may be necessary to protect women from further assault, but it may conflict with women's wish to develop healthy loving relationships with them.
★ What relationships will the centre develop with other agencies in the voluntary, commercial and state sectors?
★ What support does the group expect from the public?
  - Target the groups it intends to reach. Consider women and sympathetic men. Consider political organisations and parties, especially women's sections, women's groups, both feminist and non-feminist, community groups, labour organisations, and women sharing the experience of the group setting up the facility.
★ Make sure the relationship with supporters does not endanger egalitarian group processes and dynamics by ceding control to them.

* Methods of reaching the public include leafletting, community newspapers, public meetings, established media coverage (television, radio via interviews), articles, and lectures, the anti-establishment media, street theatre, video, direct action such as demonstrations, lobbying, squatting and occupations.
* Maintaining group morale.

Public Meetings

Public meetings can be important in the community activists' repertoire for explaining their actions to the public, particularly if it is unaware of their group's existence. These can convey information to others, mobilise support for a proposed plan of action, and lead to the formation of an umbrella organisation which can organise action around particular issues.

Though public meetings can be important vehicles for communicating to mass audiences, they can very easily go awry. Careful thought on handling the meeting, preparing for it in advance and allocating tasks to different members of the group are essential in ensuring that:

* people are notified about the meeting;
* the meeting itself is well-organised and run; and
* that the meeting achieves the aims and objectives set for it.

Identifying someone to take the minutes helps obtain an accurate recording of the proceedings for use in future deliberations. If the subject under discussion is serious or controversial, create a relaxed but sober start to the meeting. If the meeting is primarily a social occasion, make sure that everyone attending enjoys themselves. After welcoming all those present, the chairperson should explain the purpose of the meeting and how she intends to run it.

The chairperson for the meeting is a significant and powerful figure. The group must give careful consideration to whom it wants in this position. She must be able to control the meeting and apply the rules of order so that it runs smoothly, give people on the panel the opportunity to convey their messages to those attending and facilitate members of the audience gain the floor. This includes allowing those supporting and those opposing particular proposals to speak in an orderly fashion. She must also be prepared to deal with hecklers and others disrupting the proceedings. The group may wish to role-play such situations in advance, thereby empowering the chairperson in her handling of actual ones. The group may also need to consider other ways of supporting the chairperson control disruptive people.

Speakers should be given specific guidance about what they should discuss and how long they may speak at the meeting. Wherever possible, they should be given sufficient advance notice to prepare themselves fully for the task. Some women will be daunted by the prospect of speaking at a public meeting. The chairperson may need to help them deal with their nervousness. Finding ways of reducing nervousness on the night can also be role-played by the group. Speakers may supplement their contributions by using films, videos, slides or other aids to present their message more interestingly and effectively.

In planning the end of the meeting, make sure someone is allocated the task of placing suggestions and motions before participants. Also designate a person to take responsibility for summarising the main points of the meeting. Calls for action, appeals for cash and details of future meetings should be made at this point. The recruitment of new members can become inordinately long. Women will leave before the meeting finishes if they are either bored or have other commitments to fulfill. Start on time and finish on time. If the group has previously decided it is appropriate to do so, the chairperson may invite those wishing to remain once the meeting ends to chat informally over refreshments.

Leaflets

Leaflets are useful vehicles for communication between an action group and the community because they are relatively cheap and easy to produce. Leaflets can provide residents with the group's views on specific issues and give them up to date information on controversial matters. Since leaflets are intended to communicate with people, they should look well produced, and give a clear and concise message. The presentation and organisation of a leaflet should attract the reader's attention and hold it whilst the leaflet is being read. It should neither sensationalise issues nor degrade women. The following points may act as minimal guides in the production of leaflets:

★ *Be informative* Decide on the issue to be addressed, what the group wants to say about it, and to whom it should be said. Leaflets should provide people with the following information:
   – What is happening?
   – Who is doing it?
   – Where it is happening?
   – Why it is happening?
   – When it is happening?
* *Get the 'facts' right* Accuracy in the information released is essential if the group is not to lose credibility.
★ *Make the leaflet interesting* The leaflet should attract readers through its presentation as well as by what it says on particular issues. It should use a number of techniques in its layout to provide variety. It should also be easily recognisable as standing

53

for the group. Hence, an attractive symbol, a memorable abbreviation or catchy name should be used to imprint its particular message in readers minds. Headings can highlight important points or signal a transition between one message and another. Cartoons and pictures can present the group's views more graphically.

★ *Make the leaflet simple* Simplicity in presenting the message and in the language used enhances the chances of the group's message being communicated to others.

★ *Printing the leaflet* Make a mock-up of the leaflet. This gives the group the opportunity to see how it looks and reads. It can also help spot errors before printing. Printing can be an expensive process. Choose a method which is appropriate to the group's budget. Offset litho may look very professional, but can the group handle the costs? Stencil duplicating is much cheaper. Investigate the different options available for printing before the group become committed to a particular method.

★ *Distributing the leaflet* Distributing the leaflet can also cost a lot of money, unless this is undertaken by volunteers. The group needs to decide who is to receive the leaflet, and whether or not there will be a charge. Women's limited access to financial resources could be decisive here. Both considerations will be affected by whom your audience is, its relationship to the group, and the group's resources. The people distributing the leaflet should be familiar with its contents and be prepared to answer questions on the material it contains.

★ *Have a contact person* The leaflet should have the name, address and phone number of someone who is available to answer questions about the group and its position on a given matter. In Britain, the name and address of the person(s) or organisation(s) printing and publishing the leaflet must be provided as a legal requirement.

★ *Take heed of libel and copyright laws* The laws against slandering individuals apply to leaflets as to any other medium of communication. Make sure that these are not infringed. Getting the facts about any issue correct is invaluable in keeping the group out of the courts.

Community Newspapers

Producing a community newspaper provides community activists with the opportunity to use alternative methods of collecting and organising information than those prevailing in the traditional commercial press nationally or locally. Feminists organise their community newspapers collectively. In these, editorial policy and decisions about the community newspaper's production, distribution and costs are made by the editorial collective which operates on an egalitarian basis. This form of operation contrasts with the hierarchical structure under the authority of the editor guiding relationships amongst workers in the traditional press.

Another equally important feature is that those making the news also report and produce it in an easily accessible form for their audience. Therefore, it embodies a different conception of news and what is newsworthy. In a feminist production, emphasis is placed on those affected by the event being involved in communicating it to others. The notion of the dispassionate, neutral reporter presenting their case gives way to involved activist ones. Secondly, the dissemination of information and what is considered newsworthy is neither constrained nor determined by the test of profitability. Rather, the question is what information do women want to convey and what information do they require to take action. Thirdly, many editorial collectives produce community newspapers noted for their consciousness-raising potential through the provision of controversial information and points of view not normally evident in the traditional papers. Also, tasks are shared and individual women are encouraged to learn a range of skills.

The high ideals of collectively produced, non-profit oriented feminist community newspapers are difficult to establish. There are problems in sustaining continuity in the editorial collective over long periods of time, obtaining funds for launching the community newspaper and maintaining production in the long-term even if the community newspaper is distributed free and is produced by unpaid, voluntary labour. Despite these difficulties, there are examples of successful ventures in the alternative feminist press which have consolidated their position and extended their operations over a considerable time span, as has *Spare Rib*.

Points to Consider in Launching a Community Newspaper

* How will the newspaper be produced?
  – collectively or hierarchically under an editor?
* On what basis will the contents of the paper be decided?
* How often will the paper be printed?
* How will the paper be financed?
* Will there be a charge for the paper? If yes, how much?
* How will the newspaper be distributed? By whom? (paid or unpaid workers)
* How will women's involvement in the production of the newspaper be maintained?
* Technical Decisions:
  – What format will it have?
  – How will headings be used?
  – How will the front page be laid out?
  – What layout will be used?
  – What size of paper will be used?

- How many pages will the newspaper have?
- Will the paper contain photographs?
- Will the paper use cartoons?
- How will the paper be produced? (offset litho, stencil duplicating)
★ How will tasks be allocated?
★ What premises will be required to produce the paper?
★ Provide the printers address on the newspaper.
★ Beware:
  - Libelous statements.
  - Inaccurate facts.
  - Copyright regulations.

Handling the Media

Dealing with the conventional media – television, papers, radio, demands that women community activists acquire important skills. This involves their learning how to negotiate a path through the forest of incorporation, sensationalism and ridicule facing those trying to communicate radical viewpoints, present their case accurately and deal with conflict and controversy. For feminist community workers the question of handling the media is critical. Feminism's commitment to transforming social relations makes feminism an anti-establishment philosophy which is unlikely to be treated sympathetically by the conventional media. The likelihood is that feminist perspectives and points of view will be trivialised and/or sensationalised in ways that foster hostility to the feminist cause.

Many community groups have tried to deal with the dilemmas and contradictions posed by their interaction with the conventional media by developing their own alternative forms of dramatic communication, for example, street theatre, community video, *Spare Rib*. Though these forms are important in their own right, the size of the audience they can reach compared to the mass media is small. The support systems and resources underwriting the messages which can be effectively delivered through feminist ventures are also limited. It is important, therefore, that community groups are able to exploit effectively both the traditional and alternative media.

Points to Consider in Dealing with the Media

* What is considered 'newsworthy'?
  - Conflict;
  - Hardship and danger to the community;
  - Public scandal;

– Unusualness; and
– Individualism.
* How does 'newsworthiness' affect the media's response to your cause?
* Press Officer to Handle Publicity:
  – Rotated to give all women the skills.
  – Has the press officer been given clear guidelines on what to say about the campaign?
  – How does the group decide on its spokesperson for each occasion?
* Preparation (before interview/appearing on TV)
  – Roleplaying the interview with group members.
  – Collecting and verifying all the information needed.
  – Is the timing of the interview suitable?
  – How will the group's/spokesperson's arrival at the interview be handled?
  – Make a note of the main points the group wishes discussed.
  – Assess whether or not the reporter/interviewer will be sympathetic and how his/her hostility might be handled.
  – Ways of handling reporter's hostility:
    – Refusing the interview (this may result in the group being unable to present its case elsewhere);
    – Putting conditions on the interview and on how the information is going to be released (this keeps the initiative with the group);
    – Looking for other publicity (this means finding the group's own sympathetic source).
* During the Interview:
  – How do you maintain the initiative/control?
  – Define which questions you are not prepared to answer and have your reasons for doing so available for presentation, for example, protecting a vulnerable person's identity; secrecy (particularly relevant in considerations over the forms of action the group wishes to undertake); accountability to your group (you are responsible to it for both your views and your behaviour); and bad taste (Is something offensive or degrading?).
  – Consider how information the group gives will be used: Explain why you won't comment when this is your position; Be positive in your approach and your statements; Be friendly (insofar as possible; this may be difficult).
  – Beware of long questions which 'summarise' your position and require only a 'yes' or 'no' answer. It will distort your group's case.
  – Be clear about what you want to say and how you want to say it (prepare yourself beforehand).
* Don't be pushed into giving answers to impromptu questions, particularly on the phone, unless you are certain of the answer.

Ask the reporter to call back later if necessary. Otherwise, you may reveal more information than your group intended you to give.

* Comments which are 'Off the Record':
  – Such comments make reporters suspicious about what it is you are trying to hide, and should be avoided.
* If after giving an interview, you remember something else you want to say, go back to the reporter and tell him/her about it.
* Make a note of the main points of your conversation with the reporter afterwards. You may need it to check the article when it appears.
* Follow-up after the interview:
  – Check what the reporter says about your case.
  – Ask for the right of reply if you feel your case is wrongly presented.
  – Check out the reactions of the readers/your supporters to the article or report whenever possible.
* Don't go for publicity just for the sake of it. Use publicity to promote your case, not to detract from it.
* Ways of attracting publicity:
  – Press release;
  – Letters to the editor;
  – Feature articles; and
  – Taking action.

The Press Release

The Press Release is a springboard to publicity because it provides the group with an opportunity to present *its* arguments and *its* views on *its* particular campaign or action as opposed to those items identified by the media. It is an important document and must be carefully prepared so as to attract interest in the group's cause. Once this interest is secured, the group has further work to do with those responding positively (for example, by printing your press release or details contained within it) if you want further publicity to stem from it.

Points to Consider in Preparing a Press Release

★ *Purpose* What is the purpose of your press release?
  – Background information.
  – Notice of event.
  – Report of meeting/event.
  – Details of campaign.
  – Basis of interview.
★ *Newsworthiness* Is what you have to say 'newsworthy'?
★ *Style* Is your style suitable for the task?
  – Use short, simple sentences.

- Concentrate on facts.
- Use quotes from individuals involved in the campaign or work.
★ *Essential information* Your information should cover the following questions:
  - What is happening?
  - Who is doing it?
  - Where is it happening?
  - When is it happening?
  - Why is it happening?
★ *Length* Presentation and impact are affected by length.
  - Try to stick to one sheet of paper, of A4 size.
  - If possible, use headed paper. Otherwise, have the name of your organisation on the top of the paper.
  - Give the important aspects of what you are trying to say prominence.
★ *Release* Give the *date* of release clearly.
★ *Embargo* Give the *date* of when the story can be *published* if you wish the information to be held back.
  - Avoid having an embargo wherever possible. It is preferable for you to release the information later instead.
★ *Headlines* Use headlines in presenting your information, but make them short and simple.
★ *First Paragraph* The first paragraph of your press release is crucial. It should attract the reader's attention.
  - It should keep the reader's attention and interest in what the group is saying.
  - Other paragraphs follow from this, but this paragraph should set the tone of the release, and should be set-off from the rest of it.
★ *Typing* Press releases should be typed wherever possible. It makes for easier reading and it is more likely to be read.
★ *End of Press Release* The termination of the press release should be clearly marked, ENDS.
★ *Contact Person* The name and address of the contact person should be provided at the end of the press release. Give a phone number if possible.
★ *Photographs* Give details of whether or not photographs are available and if they can be used by the press.

Building a Picture of the Community: The Community Profile

A community profile is a detailed picture of a community. The knowledge it provides is a pre-requisite for effective feminist community campaigns around issues and securing external support for its activities because it reveals the people, skills and resources to be found in an area. A community profile is compiled on both an informal and a formal basis, drawing on knowledge which already exists within the community and the group that initially meets to raise consciousness around an issue. Women are a rich source of information about a community, most of which is inaccessible through formal information gathering and storing facilities.

Community activists collect details on a community when identifying the economic, political and social needs of a particular area and resources which the local inhabitants may have. Whether working solely with women or in mixed groups, feminist community workers try to ensure that data collection follows feminist principles; leaving control over the use of information with those providing it, sharing information and the skills entailed in collecting it amongst group members; highlighting the significance of gender throughout the process of data collection, dissemination and use; and utilising the findings in improving women's position (see Eichler, 1988; Kelly, 1988; Stanley and Wise, 1983; Roberts, 1985). Having collected their information, community activists should assess the accuracy of their information and the support which exists for taking action over identified issues. This can be achieved by forming groups around specified problem areas and checking out people's opinions and willingness to take action. The methods used for doing this can range from word of mouth to formal surveys. People will have varying degrees of commitment ranging from agreeing to vote in favour of an action to occupying a building.

A community profile can identify opposition to a plan of action by revealing the vested interests people have in particular positions. Knowing who the group's opponents are likely to be can facilitate action planning. It can also help when formulating counter-arguments to those which will be put by the opposition and in forming support groups.

Some of the major aims, objectives and items to be considered in developing a community profile are presented below. Compiling a community profile is a lengthy process which never really terminates since the information which is held collectively by the group must be continually updated. Some of the information required is already publicly available; some will have to be unearthed by the group. It is also important that the information making up the community profile is easily accessible to supportive community groups. Ensuring the accessibility of the profile requires the group to consider how the information can be updated, distributed and stored. Improving women's access to information enhances their manouevrability in ensuing power struggles and strengthens their willingness to challenge their current lack of information and the powerlessness which stems from it (Adamson et al., 1988).

Organising Tips

Compiling a Community Profile

Aims

- ★ To Identify community needs (where resources are required).
- ★ To identify organisational, material, human and other resources available in the community on both formal and informal levels.
- ★ To help in the presentation of the group's case for support of various forms.
- ★ To use the information collected to enhance the well-being of women, children and men.

Ultimate Uses

- ★ To organise people so that they can change their community in accordance with their needs.
- ★ To redistribute power and resources in egalitarian directions.

Major Items to be Covered

Physical Description of the Area

(These may be portrayed in audio-visual format, for example, a map)

- ★ Where is the community physically located?
- ★ What general description would you give it?
- ★ What industries, enterprises, factories, offices, workplaces, does it have and where are they located?
- ★ What shopping facilities are there and where are they located?
- ★ What recreational facilities are there and where are they located?
- ★ How is land used (include recreational land)?
- ★ What major roads and natural barriers, for example, rivers, divide the area?
- ★ Are there empty properties in the area?
  - – Where are these located?
  - – Who owns them?
- ★ What types of housing are there?
  - – According to tenure:
    - – council tenant;
    - – private tenant; and
    - – owner occupier.
- ★ What is the distribution of housing according to social divisions?

- class;
- race;
- gender, and
- age.
★ What type of housing construction is there?
  - house with gardens;
  - flats;
  - maisonettes;
  - tower blocks; and
  - communal living arrangements.
★ Where is each type of housing located?
★ What amenities do the houses have?
★ Is there overcrowding in the houses?
★ What community halls, churches, pubs, social clubs and social buildings are there?
★ What transportation networks (sea, land, rail, air) are there?
  - What is the frequency of service?
  - How much do these services cost?
★ What plans does the local authority have for the area?

Demographic Description

★ What is the gender distribution in the area?
★ What is the ethnic distribution in the area?
★ What is the age distribution in the area?
★ What is the income distribution of the people living in the area (include people on social security, pensions, unemployment benefits, waged income and inheritances)?
★ What occupations do people living in the area have?
★ How many multi-household/single parent household dwellings are there?
★ What religious practices are observed by people in the area?
★ What are the 'travel-to-work journey' distances (do people commute or work locally)?
★ How do people use their leisure time? What hobbies do they have?

Economic Description

★ Who are the employers in the area?
  - Where do they live?
  - What are their life-styles?
★ How many employees does each employer have?
  - Are they organised in trade unions, company associations, or are they unorganised?
  - What are employers attitudes to these organisations?
★ Are the employers making a profit?
  - What plans do they have for remaining in the area?

62

- What attracted them to the area in the first instance (for example, subsidies, available labour, cheap land, cheap premises)?
★ What future plans for developing the local economy are there?
  - Are new employers coming into the area?
  - Where?
  - How many jobs do they offer?
  - Where do these employers come from (they often disinvest in other deprived areas to go to one which offers more profit making incentives including public subsidies and cheap labour)?
★ What do councillors/government officers think of these developments?
★ Can the local authority/central state take a more interventionist role in promoting the community's future well-being?
  - At what points?
  - For what purposes?
  - How?

Political Description

★ Which political parties, organisations are involved in the community?
★ How does this compare to their involvement in other parts of the city?
★ What have they done (not done) for the community?
★ What resources do these political parties and organisations have at their disposal?
★ What is the relationship between these organisations and the residents like (include their power base and the number of supporters they have)?
★ Which trade unions are active in the area and how?
  - What resources do they have at their disposal?
  - Are these available to the community?
★ Which community groups and organisations are there?
  - How many people do each of these contain?
  - What policies do they hold?
  - What campaigns have they had?
  - Who leads them or organises their activities?
  - What resources do they have?
★ Which feminist organisations including campaigns and networks can you identify in the community?
  - What resources do they have available?
  - How can you gain their support for your group's activities?

Informal Networks

★ Who is looked up to for advice/opinion formation?

* What is their power base and the extent of their power (this may be informal)?
* What views do they hold strongly?
* Who is the neighbourhood 'gossip' and why?
* Who is the neighbourhood 'scapegoat' and why?
* What voluntary organisations are there, for example, churches, charities?
* What specialist groups are there, for example, groups for elders, single parents, handicapped people, disabled people, and unemployed people?
* Who runs these groups?
  – What resource do they have?
  – What activities do they support?
  – How easy is it for new members to join?
* Who are their supporters?
  – What views/opinions do they endorse?
* Are there any informal 'helping' networks, for example, helping the old, the sick?
  – Who does the helping?
  – Who runs the groups?
  – Which groups of residents do they help?
  – How do they help these groups?
  – Where do the helpers and the people they help live?

Information Collection

The collection of this information is necessary for community activists to enable them to:

* Become accepted as organisers.
* Understand a community.
* Become involved in organising that community.

The information may be collected in a variety of ways. Some of these include:

Impressionistic Enquiry

This is most useful for community activists wanting an easily and quickly obtained impression of the community in which they are involved. It is also the cheapest method of information collection. The method is basically informal and relies on community activists talking to, listening to and watching community residents and groups or organisations with which they wish to interact. At this point, community activists are 'sussing out' the community and getting to know it. The community is simultaneously becoming informed about them. The main drawbacks in this method are:

* The community worker is dependent on the items people are willing to reveal to an 'outsider'.
* The skills and powers of observation of the community activist may introduce bias ignoring important subtleties into the picture.

The 'impressions' obtained may be very fragmented and lack a coherent structure for recognising significant processes operating in the situation; the interaction between the community activist and the community can assume a one-dimensional image. The main advantages of an impressionistic enquiry is that one can develop a 'picture' of the community in a relatively short time span. It is a cheap method to finance as few resource commitments are necessary, and it relies on community activists utilising their intuitive capacities and exercising their judgements.

Opinion Surveys

Questionnaires or interviews are useful in ascertaining peoples' views and opinions on issues. Feminists have varied traditional approaches to these by intensively exploring issues through a small number of interviews. In these the 'researcher' uses her experience as a woman to develop a rapport with the women being interviewed (Stanley and Wise, 1983). This provides insights not usually accessible through traditional approaches. Additionally, the women being interviewed are given some control over the results of the research which must be used to promote women's interests (Kelly, 1988). Feminists may also use more traditional survey methods, though omitting their most sexist elements by introducing gender as an explicit variable (Eichler, 1988). The sensitivity to gender issues and an awareness of the different ways in which gender affects men and women make feminist approaches to research in the community valid for both men and women. Feminists do not administer opinion surveys in a vacuum, but as part of a programme of action. The main weakness of the survey approach stems from the extent to which skeptics will accept the survey's generalisability. It may reflect people's attitudes at the time of the survey, but these may undergo change as other variables in the situation change. The basis on which the survey sample is selected introduces its own bias. However, opinion surveys enable community activists to test reactions to proposed programmes before they are implemented. Opinion surveys also act as a means whereby suggestions for programmes of action can be obtained before the plan of action is fully developed. In developing their community profile, community activists need skills to enable them to sensitively use available resources for collecting information on who interacts with whom, in which locations, and for what purposes.

Local Sources of Information

★*Local libraries* are useful in providing local histories of the area.
Information on the role of local firms and local politicians in the
devleopment of the local socio-economic system can be obtained
here. However, the material may exclude women's contribution,
and you may need to rely on oral histories, particularly for
working class and black women.

★*Local Community Groups* often have a lot of useful information on
the local personalities and community perceptions of them.

★*Local Newspapers* are very revealing of community interaction, not
just in feature articles, but in the small items. These often
indicate which people have social contact with others. A systematic collection of this information enables community activists to
construct a pattern of interactions which can inform their activities.

Formal Sources

★*Census data*

★*Town plans*

★*Company reports, company papers, and company officers*, can provide
details on company organisation, including subsidiary companies,
investment policies, employment policies and decision-making
mechanisms. Useful quotes may also be gleaned during this
exercise. Also, public relations officers at the local level and head
office are other useful sources of information.

★ *Companies House, the Registrar of Friendly Societies, the Charities
Commission*, can all supply the minimal information that commercial enterprises are legally required to divulge. The information obtained from their records must be treated carefully since
it is incomplete. The omissions can be as important as the
revelations. Additional information on commercial enterprises,
their nature and the activities in which they are involved can
be acquired from the following sources:

> *Who Owns Whom*
> *U.K. Compass*
> *Register of British Industry and Commerce*
> *Moodie Cards (Moodie's Company Service)*
> *Kelly's Directory*
> *Register of Business Names*
> *Stock Exchange Register of Defunct Companies*
> *Extel Book of New Issues (Stocks)*.

Community activists must be able to develop a coherent analysis from this rather fragmented collection of information. Feminist community workers use a feminist perspective in making sense
of this data, but other community workers rely on their political

philosophies. This perspective provides the spine structuring the information that is procured.

Use of Information

Producing a report based on the information gathered and not followed through by action is of little significance to the community. Information, particularly information countering that provided by the media and the official bureaucracy, can become a critical element in the community's struggle to fulfill its perceived needs. In writing a pamphlet or report, community activists have to consider the audience they are addressing. An expensively produced, highly abstract or technological (jargonistic) pamphlet will not motivate local working class community organisations to either read the publication or involve themselves in action predicated on it. The publication must speak their language and address their reality in concrete terms for it to be an effective means of communication and galvanizer of action.

The tactical use of the information collected requires serious consideration. Some situations will call for the slow release of information so as to get the other side to provide further details of its activities. Other situations may demand the immediate release of information collected. In any event, the use of the information becomes a political function. Politically used information can become a threat to the *status quo*. Because of this, community activists must ensure the accuracy of their 'facts'. Otherwise the whole weight of the legal apparatus pertaining to libel and slander may be brought to bear against their group, or they may find both they and their group lose credibility.

Chapter 3
Feminist Action on the Individual Level

As individuals, women have a very personal experience of oppression. Feminists have sought to develop a theory and practice which responds to women's individual suffering as well as trying to eliminate collective hardship. Feminist therapy and work in feminist health collectives have been central to developing feminists response to individual women.

This chapter examines feminist action on the individual level. It focuses on the use feminists have made of consciousness-raising in individual work and with small groups to highlight the connections between individual women's plight and their subordination socially (Howell and Bayes, 1981). Feminist therapy and feminist self-help groups in the health field are major developments drawing upon feminists' work with individuals in consciousness-raising groups. Besides building up women's sense of confidence and mastery in challenging professions which have been bastions of male privilege, these activities have provided women with resources in the community which women have created and can control. As such they prefigure the egalitarian social relations which feminists strive to attain and offer concrete examples of the ways in which feminists make connections between an individual woman's position and the social forces within which her life is elaborated. This chapter will also provide guidelines for setting up consciousness-raising and feminist self-help groups.

Feminist Approaches to Women's Emotional Well-Being

Feminist work with individual women in counselling and therapy sessions reveals how important it is for women to make the connections between their personal predicament and the social context within which they live, if the emotional damage in their existence is to be repaired. Their work has revealed the pervasiveness of women's feelings of powerlessness and the psychological and emotional sacrifices women make living up to the demands placed on them by the community's traditional definitions of femininity (Howell and Bayes, 1981). Depression, frustrated hopes and ambitions, feelings of uselessness and lack of worth, all feature in their responses to the circumscribed lives women are compelled to lead. Working with women on the personal level has revealed the social origins of women's poor emotional health and uncovered the distortion in women's emotional lives caused by their having to adhere to feminine stereotypes (Baker Miller, 1978; Howell and Bayes, 1981). Poverty, bad housing, unremitting childcare, and arduous elder care take their toll on women's emotional welfare (Brown and Harris, 1978; Howell and Bayes, 1981) and are central in constructing women's experience of lack of fulfillment and emotional powerlessness. The flashes of joy women experience in their relationships with their children and others, occur within a context of constant anxieties about their own and their children's physical and emotional well-being. Feminists have rejected analyses which pathologise women who respond to their situation with mental illness, drug abuse, alcohol abuse, or excessive smoking, and point instead to the material and emotional deprivation which women are having to manage daily. Offering women support in building a positive sense of self; highlighting the connections between low self-esteem, the roles women are expected to play, and the resources they have at their disposal; and examining the nature of women's relationships with other women and men; are important dimensions in feminist work at the individual level. Additionally, feminists' approach to emotional work has lessened the stigma attached to seeking counselling advice.

In the therapeutic relationship fostered through feminist therapy, women are encouraged to examine the social causes of their personal suffering and examine the ways in which these have contributed to their feelings of worthlessness and self-denigration. The exploration of their psychological development draws on the experiences they share with other women and their feminist therapist (Howell and Bayes, 1981). A feminist therapist bases her empathy with and understanding of the woman's situation on her own experience of oppression as a woman. This lays the groundwork for relating to the woman in less remote, impersonal and hierarchical ways than is the case in traditional therapeutic relationships which rely on a professional distance being maintained in the client-worker relationship. Feminism challenges the prevailing definition of professionalism and redefines it in more egalitarian directions. The feminist therapist is there to listen to the woman's account of her position and work with her to make sense of its contradictory elements, and her own dissatisfaction with her performance (Marchant and Wearing, 1986). In this way, feminist therapy enables women to grow in confidence and make decisions for themselves. The development of such a relationship between the woman and the therapist cannot be assumed. It needs to be worked at. Moreover, there may be other forms of oppression besides gender invading the therapeutic relationship for feminist therapists to confront, for example, racism. White therapists need to examine very carefully the extent to which they can empathise with black women whose experience of sexism is substantially different from theirs. Even black feminist therapists working with black women have to work hard to overcome the abyss which racism places between them (see Lorde, 1984).

Feminist therapy is not underpinned by notions imbued with the subordination of women as is therapy following Freudian understandings (Dominelli and McLeod, 1989). This enables women to develop a healthy respect and liking for other women and makes it easier for women to begin relating to other women without the competition, envy and jealousy characterising many of the women-to-women relationships in society more generally. This can also lay the basis for women looking to other women for emotional fulfillment in both loving and working relationships. In other words, women begin to move away from their dependency on men for the validation of their existence and place in society, and replace it with a sense of independence and self-reliance, which can seek support from others without feeling that their world is caving in if support or approval is denied. According to Eichenbaum and Orbach (1982; 1984), feminist therapy enables women to feel worthy and deserving of attention and confirms their entitlement to receiving love, care and affection in the process. This contrasts sharply with traditional expectations that women are only givers of love, care and affection. Fostering women's strengths and beliefs in themselves is a vital part of the process of feminist therapy. Women who have worked on their problems through feminist therapy have claimed that it has reduced their sense of powerlessness (Ernst and Maquire, 1987; McLeod, 1987) and enabled them to reject the victim role. Moreover, these women have found that the work they have pursued in feminist therapy sessions has been directly relevant for their everyday lives, thereby making it easier for them to incorporate the lessons they have learnt and skills they have acquired into their routine activities (Heenan, 1988; McLeod, 1987). This has in turn made them feel more in control of their domestic and where applicable, waged working lives.

Therapies founded on Freudian premises focus on the father-daughter/male-female relationship as the fundamental one in personality formation (Freud, 1977). Feminist therapy focuses on developing women's understanding of their relationships with other significant women in their lives. The crucial one in this respect is the mother-daughter relationship which forms the centrepiece of object relations theory (Eichenbaum and Orbach, 1982; 1984; Ernst and Maguire, 1987). This approach has yielded a significant shift away from male supremacy as the underpinning of professionals' understanding of women's condition and pyschological development. However, there is a danger that feminist therapy has focused too exclusively on the mother-daughter relationship as a reaction against its neglect in Freudian psychology, and ignored crucial others in women's lives. For example, black women have an experience of important bonding taking place with a range of extended family members, including grandmothers and aunts rather than developing an exclusive relationship with their mothers (Wilson, 1977; Bryan *et al*, 1985). It may be that prevailing object relations theory is only valid for certain groups of white women who were raised in nuclear family set-ups. A sensitivity to the impact of racism on black women's lives would make feminists question the universal applicability of such an analysis. Additionally, the Eichenbaum and Orbach (1982, 1984) approach to the mother-daughter relationship carries the danger of unwittingly contributing to blaming mothers for failing to socialise their daughters into leading independent lives.

The Eichenbaum and Orbach (1982, 1984) position also leaves out crucial questions which a feminist analysis has to address if it is going to eliminate gender oppression. These include questions about the nature of the relationships between men and women. What kind of socialisation process is appropriate for the development of egalitarian relations between men and women, whether they are relating to them as intimate partners or as colleagues at work? What role should men play in childrearing? That is, how do we, as feminists, challenge the prevailing definition of fathering (which is limited largely to the biological act of impregnating women, and the economic act of providing for the material welfare of unwaged mothers and their children) and redefine it in ways that are more conducive to the kind of fathering relationship that fosters the emotional well-being of children, women and men? Finally, feminists also have to ask questions about women's role in socialising male children in anti-sexist ways in the mother-son relationship and their waged work with children, be it in the schools, the health service, the media or other public arena. To what extent do women pass on sexist stereotypes to their sons or pupils because they have internalised the values and norms of a society celebrating male supremacy? How do we raise boy children so that they work for rather than undermine women's liberation. Asking these questions is not to blame women for being unable to operate outside of the patriarchal context in which their lives are elaborated, for the whole of the feminist struggle is aimed at creating non-oppressive social relations which will transcend patriarchy. But it is necessary to put forward these queries if we are to understand fully the complexity of the task which we as feminists are undertaking, and to ensure that our gains in one arena will not be undermined by the absence of progress in other arenas which intricately interconnect with the particular aspect of social relations being addressed. These questions must also be asked if feminist therapy is not to slip into supporting women and strengthening their self-esteem by denigrating the need of children and men for emotional fulfillment.

The growing literature on the sexual abuse of children signifies the horrific subordination of their emotional well-being to that of men (Ward, 1984; Armstrong, 1987; Nelson, 1982; Dominelli, 1986a). Though girls are their major victims, boys are also being sexually abused by adult men. Women can only ignore men's exploitation of children at the expense of their commitment to developing egalitarian relationships amongst all members of society. Men's lack of emotional fulfillment is also coming to light as a result of feminist work and has led men to begin challenging dominant notions of masculinity (Bowl, 1985; Tolson, 1978; Festau, 1975; Achilles' Heel Collective, 1983; Hearn, 1987). Black men and women are finding their right to emotional fulfillment threatened by racist immigration laws which deny them access to their families (Plummer, 1978; Gordon and Newnham, 1985); and poor job prospects, bad housing and other forms of racism which deny them access to the material conditions necessary for ensuring emotional growth (Davis, 1989). Additionally, racist practices permeate every aspect of their lives to the detriment of their emotional development. Internalised racism takes its toll by undermining black people's sense of identity, pride in their historical achievements and resistance to racism (Gilroy, 1987; Comer and Poussaint, 1975; Coard, 1971). Black women have also found that racism has destroyed extended family networks, increased their isolation in society thereby denying them a voice in its affairs (Wilson, 1977), and distorted the close relationships they can establish with other black women (Lorde, 1984).

The emotional sphere is also one in which feminists have uncovered a multi-layered tissue of violence absorbing the psychic energies of children, women, and men and seriously impoverishing their emotional lives. Routine violence is exercised over children by both men and women in the name of disciplining and socialising them into their role in life (Miller, 1983). Male perpetrated violence is an inescapable fact of women's lives in the home, factory, office and on the streets (Kelly, 1988). White man's responsibility in both reproducing these oppressive and damaging relations and eradicating them is deflected by playing on racist stereotypes and focusing attention on black men (Davis, 1989; Bryan *et al*, 1985). Yet, most attacks on women, black and white, are committed by white men (Davis, 1989). The world sits poised on an arsenal of nuclear weapons which can be set off at any time. Women's fears about the safety of their children, their families and their sense of powerlessness in an increasingly militarised world have added to the emotional pressures they face. This has led feminists to redefine violence, not only as physical damage but also as a climate of fear created by men without using physical weapons causing psychological damage which is just as pernicious as visible wounds and bruises. This climate of fear of male attack has penetrated the consciousness of all women whether or not they have been physically beaten and humiliated by men for all women have to take precautions which will minimise the likelihood of an attack actually happening (Brownmiller, 1976). Having to presume that an attack will occur unless women take active steps to prevent it has operated as an effective form of patriarchal social control and has enabled society, especially through the courts and legal process, to blame women when an attack takes place, for example, victim blaming in rape (see Brownmiller, 1976; Kelly, 1988; Scottish Women's Aid Federation, 1980). The extent to which men are absolved of responsibility in this matter and the burden of guilt for failed self-protection imposed on women who have been unable to stop their attacker was recently evident in a Canadian court case in which a judge gave a male child molester a suspended sentence because he was 'provoked by a sexually aggressive three year old (girl) child'! (*The Vancouver Sun*, 1989).

Women have felt compelled to reasses their views about violence – its inevitability as something natural; their powerlessness in stemming its pervasiveness; and its distortion of personal and public life. In America, the feminist peace movement has challenged the priorities of a society in which 60 cents out of every income-tax dollar is appropriated by the Pentagon (Davis, 1989) whilst children are suffering from malnutrition, women are homeless on the streets, and men endanger their health producing armaments. Feminists have linked increased defence expenditures under Reagan to the devastation of state welfare services, particularly Aid to Families With Dependent Children, Medicaid and Medicare, health services to the poor and older people respectively, and education (Davis, 1989). The feminist peace movement has highlighted the extent to which community life could be enhanced if defence resources were channelled into welfare expenditure. America could develop a national comprehensive health care service; fund a guaranteed income for all poor Americans; or finance basic health supplies for millions of children in the Third World. In England, the feminist peace movement has made similar connections by exposing the deleterious effects the fear of nuclear war has had on individual women and children's emotional well-being, and the waste of public resources entailed in a strategy of escalating nuclear weaponry (Cook and Kirk, 1983).

Advocacy: a Basis for Individual and Collective Action

Feminists have used advocacy in improving the plight of women individually and collectively as part of their strategy in initiating social change. According to Doress and Siegal (1989) advocacy comes in four forms:

* *Personal Advocacy* Under this form of advocacy, an individual woman takes action which defends her rights. For example, a woman lodging an unfair dismissal claim under the Sex Discrimination Act against her employer who sacks her for becoming pregnant. Although this action is aimed at securing justice for one individual, her defence of her rights deters the infringement of others' rights. As such, personal advocacy supports social change.
* *Interpersonal Advocacy* This form of advocacy occurs when one woman supports another who has been unfairly treated obtain justice. For example, an older woman denied disability benefits on the grounds that her crippling arthritis is not serious enough is devastated and feels there is no way in which she can alter her situation. She is not well enough to work and she has no independent financial means. Another woman, seeing her in a distraught state offers to support her in challenging the decision by appealing it. She becomes involved in preparing the case with the disabled woman and attends the hearing with her. The act of challenging injustice strengthens both women and enables them to contribute in their own way to the project of ending discrimination against older disabled women.
* *Cooperative Group Advocacy* Cooperative group advocacy involves a group of women supporting each other in dealing with problems they encounter as a group. For example, a group of older women wanting to discuss the effects of ageism with a group of younger women set up a workshop for this purpose. Each older woman is asked to bring a younger woman to the workshop. During the workshop, each woman talks about the kind of older woman she wants to be. Sharing fears about getting old, being a burden if others have to care for them in ill health, and material hardship in old age enables women to contribute to each other's understanding of their own fears and put these into context alongside similar fears being expressed by others in the group. The insights gained have enabled women to create solidarity amongst themselves and use their newfound strength in promoting the interests of older women (Doress and Siegal, 1989).
* *Organisational and Legislative Advocacy* In this form of advocacy, links are developed between groups of women with particular interests and the broader women's movement. This style of advocacy has featured in older women's contribution to feminist social action. Older women have struggled to get the government to recognise that its policies on older people, particuiarly those on pensions and social security benefits, have a differential impact on men and women. They have also had to convince

younger feminists to take their issues seriously (Doress and Siegal, 1988). Their efforts are beginning to bear fruit as together, older women's organisations and the feminist movement press for legislative and other changes to enhance the quality of older women's lives. Such developments are more advanced in the USA than in Britain (see Doress and Siegal, 1989) where the Retirement Equity Act has been passed and mandatory retirement has been abolished as a result of such alliances. The needs of older black women have been particularly neglected (Norman, 1985). This remains a pressing issue for feminist community action to address in the interests of promoting equality for black women. By organising support for older women demanding organisational and legislative changes, younger women also safeguard their future interests when they become 'older' women.

Organising Tips

Advocating for Change

Advocacy of whatever type combines an element of self-help with the attempt to achieve social change. It is, therefore, an important tool in the task of eradicating gender oppression. The following offer some guidelines which may assist in the process.
* Choose the issue to be tackled. Your problem is likely to. be shared by many others who have a similar one.
* Talk the problem through with other women and consider ways in which you can turn your problem into an issue which others unconnected to it can support.
* Define your plan of action:
  – If legislative changes are required, make sure you understand the parliamentary agenda, how to organise parliamentary support for your proposal; and know what resources are available.

Women in the Community Challenge Health Professionals

The feminist health movement has sought to combine concern with women's emotional well-being with an equal interest in their physical welfare (Doyal, 1985; Ruzek, 1978). This is in keeping with the feminist view that women's lives form an indissolvable whole which cannot be separated into discrete parts independent of each other. Every aspect of women's lives interconnects with every other aspect and accounts for the complexity in which women's oppression is embedded. The feminist health movement is largely a network of diverse health groups ministering to women's specific emotional and physical health needs. It can be called upon to campaign around issues when the need arises.

Health groups tend to be small, and have a strong consciousness-raising dimension enabling women to explore the political facets of health care at the individual and the societal level. Gender is a key element in their analysis. Besides the consciousness-raising feature, health groups also provide women with the opportunity to learn about their bodies and pass on specialist knowledge to each other. As part of a network, one health group can refer women to other groups that provide a specialist service in a particular sphere of health care. Characteristically, their work enables women to:

* Share experiences, knowledge and feelings.
* Learn from each other.
* Work on practical matters relating to health, e.g., self-examinations.
* Ask questions of themselves, other women and professionals.
* Support one another.
* Acquire confidence in tackling health issues, including resisting the authoritarian doctor-patient relationship.
* Demand more appropriate health care services.
* Change the nature of service delivery in the formal health system.
* Foster egalitarian relationships between women, regardless of their roles as providers or users of health care services.
* Work collectively with other women.
* Focus on preventative care.
* Integrate women's emotional and physical well-being.

Feminists have argued that the right to health ought to be a universally recognised human right rather than a commodity sold to those which can pay the highest price (Davis, 1989). A broader definition of health – the pursuit of health in body, mind and spirit, has featured strongly in women's struggle for economic, social and political justice (Davis, 1989; Lorde, 1988). Feminists have defined health as 'well-being which can be achieved only in a dynamic relationship with a positive and balanced environment' (Cochrane et al, 1982). This includes physical surroundings, political, economic and social structures – in short the whole way in which life is organised and our role within it elaborated. Women's attempts to challenge the power of the medical profession and make their broader definition of health care a reality through self-help initiatives have produced the women's health movement. It has picked up on issues related to women's own and their children's ill-health, and developed alternative forms of health care which have given women command of both their bodies and their treatment (Ruzek, 1978 and 1986; Doyal, 1979 and 1985). The feminist health movement has drawn on women's traditional skills in this area. Health care has been normally defined as 'women's work' except that the rise of state and market provisions has converted health to a commodity according men control (Cochrane et al, 1982; Eisenstein, 1984). Power relationships in the British National Health Service (NHS) exemplify male-female roles with the expert knowing everything whilst workers' and patients' practical experience is discounted (Cochrane et al, 1982).

Health issues enable women to explore the profound link between the personal and the political. However, this is often hidden with health and illness individualised and trivialised in the process. The traditional handling of health issues in capitalist countries has not attached importance to the social factors producing ill-health amongst various groups in society. This relationship was the focus of mass health campaigns in China immediately after the Revolution and in the creation of the *barefoot doctor* system (Sidel and Sidel, 1977; Horn, 1969) which aimed to address the health needs of women (Andors, 1983).

Black women have been particularly active in making the links between their individual poor health and the poverty structuring their lives. In America, the absence of a national health care scheme, has left them personally very vulnerable for many cannot afford hospital health insurance. Those who have purchased it have found that white administrators handling their reception into hospitals have disbelieved their claims about cover and refused them admission, thereby causing untold suffering and death (Davis, 1989). In Britain, working class women suffer from an 'illness-promoting environment', but middle class women feature more prominently in the development of feminist self-help alternatives (Cochrane et al, 1982). Working class women have played a key role in defending the NHS from the public expenditure cuts, mounting campaigns in the community and in the workplace. Women workers, particularly nurses in the NHS, have fought to improve service provision as well as get recognition of the value of their work through decent pay and conditions (Joyce et al, 1987).

Women's health groups have drawn on community action techniques during their formation. Word of mouth, door-knocking, notices strategically placed in places frequented by women have brought small numbers of women together to examine a variety of health issues. These have included childbirth, skin complaints, thrush, breast cancer, menopause, ageing, tranquillizer abuse, mental health, safety in the home, children's health. Proceeding from their own experience of the subject, such groups have raised women's consciousness about the social organisation of health. These groups often meet in women's homes, schools, or community halls with few resources other than those they provide themselves. Occasionally, they receive public funding to attract speakers or provide specialist resources. For example, the creation of Well-Women Clinics has relied on public funding. But, reliance on state financing has often imposed restrictions on the ways in which groups function, and the premises on which they base their action. This can disadvantage groups seeking to promote feminist approaches to health issues, distorting their commitment to egalitarian practices in the process (Finch, 1982; Foster, 1989). Women's health groups are also fluid in composition and in the subject matter they handle. Although a 'core' of women may remain in a group for some time, others enter and leave the group frequently, without unduly disrupting group processes. The capacity of such groups to accept turnover in membership is facilitated by the sharing of personal experiences, the relaxed atmosphere which prevails in them, the lack of hierarchical group organisation, and an understanding of the pressures which women have to negotiate in order to be free to attend such meetings. As a result, groups:

> sometimes shrink in numbers, but this is not accompanied by the frustrated bafflement it occasions in many community groups. Members know more about why people have left. They also understand more about how to bring in new people and help them settle in. Thus the group remains open.' (Cochrane *et al*, 1982:123).

The openness of groups and the commitment to egalitarian relationships has attracted women who do not normally participate in such gatherings. Having women-only groups also facilitates women's participation in group activities (South Wales Association of Tenants, 1982). Although men who work at home caring for children and retired men have joined some women's health groups without seeking to dominate group dynamics, women have preferred to keep their health groups as women-only groups (Cochrane *et al*, 1982). Meanwhile, male partners find it difficult to accept that being part of a women's health group can enhance women's well-being to the extent that they go home feeling 'happy and relaxed' (Cochrane *et al*, 1982),.

Women's health groups have stimulated relationships between women and enabled them to contribute to each other's emotional growth. They have fostered women's confidence in their ability and capacity to ask questions of professionals and the services they offer. This has also been extended to questioning the type of services which health care professionals offer to users and raised demands that health resources whether provided by the state or the market be used to further people's well-being rather than merely responding to symptoms which doctors seek to cure through high technology based interventions (Ruzek, 1978; Doyal, 1985; Cochrane *et al*, 1982). Developing preventative services which keep people healthy has been a major outcome of the feminist health movement (Foster, 1989; Ruzek, 1978; Doyal, 1985).

Additionally, women's involvement in health groups has had repercussions in other aspects of their lives. Personal relationships and the sexism within them come under scrutiny, enabling women to draw connections between these and their psychological well-being. Depression within heterosexual relationships, the toil of unremitting childcare on women's emotional health have all been related to the unsatisfactory way in which family relationships are socially structured, for these poorly serve the emotional needs of children, women and men. Group members have gained the confidence to tackle these problems more imaginatively in their personal lives, finding that they may have to break off certain relationships in the process, and demand more sensitive collective caring facilities for children and older people. Thus feminists action begun in the area of health has demonstrated the connections which exist between it and other aspects of women's lives, thereby highlighting the seamless web woven by gender oppression.

The relationships between community workers and group members in feminist health groups follow non-hierarchical principles of organisation. Tasks are shared between women, often on a rotating basis so that all women have the opportunity to learn new skills. This includes answering the telephone, chairing meetings, writing leaflets, or speaking to the media. If the process of imparting skills to one another is successful, feminist community workers find that they have become redundant to the group as it is capable of functioning without them (Cochrane et al, 1982; Dominelli, 1982). However, unconscious bids for leadership and hanging on to roles when other women have gained skills in them can mar the establishment of egalitarian relationships (Cochrane et al, 1982). A commitment to continual self-analysis and listening to other women's accounts of the group experience are essential in countering inegalitarianism and maintaining women's willingness to remain in the group. Some women's health groups resist identifying themselves with the women's movement even though they may be founded on feminist principles, operate on feminist lines, and call on the services of feminist community workers (Cochrane et al, 1982) for fear of being labelled militant, lesbian, and aggressive. The unsympathetic portrayal of feminist action in the media, and the inadvertant exclusion of certain groups of women, particularly working class and black women, by white middle class feminists have also contributed to this reaction. This indicates the extent to which feminists still have to perform a major educational task in furthering society's understanding of them and their activities, and work to develop responses taking the differences structuring gender oppression in the lives of different groups of women. Handling differences on the basis of equality and using women's different starting points to develop a common strategy in eliminating sexism is a relatively new experience for women. But the process of working for unity amongst women in a way that does not establish hierarchies whereby one type of oppression subsumes another has begun (Dominelli and McLeod, 1989).

Feminists challenge to the medical profession through the health movement has been considerable. They have questioned the patriarchal doctor-patient relationship, the skewing of medical services towards curative care that treats symptoms and promotes high technology hospital care which leaves patients feeling powerless, the distortion of health service delivery by the interests of multinational drug companies seeking profits, the abuse of women's bodies, particularly those of black women for experimental purposes and eugenicist population control, and the restriction of medical knowledge in the hands of the 'professionals' (Sidel, 1986; Bryan *et al*, 1985; Spallone and Steinberg, 1987). Childbirth and gynaecological examinations have been key sites in the battle raging between feminists and the medical profession over the best kind of health care for women. The response of the medical establishment to this challenge has not been encouraging. In America, doctors took feminists to court for illegally practising medicine by encouraging women to carry out their own gynaecological examinations (Ruzek, 1978). A massive defence of this practice by feminist groups across the country ensured that the courts accepted the feminist case. In Britain, a senior hospital obstetrician, Wendy Savage was dismissed in 1985 for incompetence after her male colleagues objected to her attempts to give women a greater say in the birth process (Savage and Leighton, 1986). By organising direct action including mass protests, conferences and a defence fund, feminists have played a key role in demanding her reinstatement and defending her right to practise sensitively in ways giving women control over their bodies. These examples depict the vulnerability of feminists attempting to challenge traditional medical practice, and the importance of having a supportive mass movement which can underwrite individual women's initiatives. They also reveal the intensely political nature of feminist intervention in the health arena.

There have been some very protracted and widely supported struggles over health issues since the late 1970s. This has led to the formation of campaigns around health issues as well as work at the individual level. In Britain, such campaigns have included preventing the closure of the Hounslow Hospital; averting the closure of the Elisabeth Garrett Anderson Hospital (EGA), one of only three women-only hospitals in the country; terminating the use of private pay-beds in the NHS hospitals; exposing the inordinate use of drugs to treat depression amongst women; and asserting women's right to control their own fertility and the health care associated with that (Rosenthal, 1983).

Women have taken a leading role in health campaigns. Women constitute the bulk of the work-force in the health service, though they are primarily located in the lowest rungs of the labour hierarchy (Doyal, 1983). Health provisions for women are also inadequate and substantially under-resourced as the feminist critique of them has revealed. Yet women's facilities and women workers have borne the brunt of public expenditure cuts in the health service. Under these circumstances, it is not surprising that women are active participants in the defence of the community's health provisions.

Struggles over health issues have provided useful lessons on organisational problems which must be overcome for a successful outcome to these campaigns. The record to date is mixed. Overall, the health service has been cut savagely under the Tories (Iliffe, 1985). But, at the local level, many facilities have been retained as a result of struggles women have waged in their defence.

Community activists can take comfort, however, from the organisational achievements of these campaigns. The Hounslow and the Elisabeth Garrett Anderson Hospital Campaigns have laid the groundwork for a broad based commitment to save these facilities. Professional workers and manual workers combined forces to oppose government policy by occupying buildings, demonstrating, lobbying the Area Health Authority, writing petitions, and seeing MPs. They have also secured financial and material resources to care for the patients left within their care, despite intense coercion by their employers and management. Trade unionists across the board have rallied support. Individuals who have never before taken part in direct action have done so for the first time to defend their perception of an essential part of the welfare state.

These campaigns have also acted as a springboard for a national offensive against the public expenditure cuts through the formation of the Fightback Campaign which organised nationally and locally. Besides promoting direct action, the Fightback Campaign has been involved in consciousness-raising endeavours through the production of its newspaper, films and speakers which can be hired by community groups fighting local battles. These have aimed to stimulate discussion about the type of health service people really want; how health rather than sickness can become its top priority; and how they can influence its decision-making processes. In short, they have made people aware that alternatives to existing provisions can and do exist. A major weakness of the Fightback Campaign has been that although it has drawn heavily on feminist ideals and practice in the women's health movement and literature, women have been excluded from the higher reaches of this Campaign. This state of affairs can be attributed in part to the inputs which have been made by the male dominated trade union movement and Left political parties.

Another important feature of the Fightback Campaign and the women's health movement operating throughout the country, is that they have raised the political questions concerning health to the top of the agenda. These have challenged the existing medical hierarchy dominated by male professionals at the apex of the medical care pyramid predicated on the subordination of women staff and patients (Doyal, 1979; Ruzek, 1978). Feminists have questioned the relevance of high technology medicine for the majority of people's illnesses, and the usefulness of a service concentrating on illness rather than health (Doyal, 1983). Finally, feminists have demanded that consumers be actively involved in making decisions about the way in which the service is organised, the facilities it provides, and the financing of the service. Through such participation, it is hoped that a democratic health service, responsible to the needs of people and emphasising prevention rather than cure, can be developed.

Organising Tips

Forming Consciousness-Raising (CR) Groups

* *Key Features*
  – Woman-centredness.
    – Meeting with other women.
    – Listening to other women.
    – Sharing experience with other women.
  – Small sized groups.
  – Redefining social problems from a feminist perspective.
  – Examining women's individual experience in a collective setting.
  – Providing women with support in confronting problems that face them individually and collectively.
  – Promoting women's confidence and strengths as women.
  – Endorsing egalitarian relations and group dynamics.
  – Making the 'personal' political.
  – Developing feminist politics and a collective approach in resolving the problem.
* *Organising a Consciousness-Raising Group*
  – Finding women to join the group:
    – Approaching women in their homes, places where they congregate, through personal contacts and networking, leafletting, posting signs, placing adverts in local papers, and forming caucuses in unions or other professional associations.
    – Meeting in places easily accessible to women including disabled women.
    – Encouraging men to facilitate women's participation in CR groups by providing supportive assistance such as childminding.

★ *Running a Consciousness-Raising Group*:
 - Timing meetings at times when women can attend most easily.
 - Structured versus Unstructured Meetings:
   - Leadership roles should be rotated amongst members; Structureless groups are usually problematic as informal hierarchies seem to establish themselves (Dreifus, 1973).
   - Focusing on issues which women themselves feel are important; having women-determined agendas and establishing these in advance of the meeting usually facilitate discussion amongst women (Curno *et al*, 1982).
 - Establishing egalitarian group processes.
   - Sensitivity to privileges, differential access to resources, and other forms of inequality between women and seeking ways of overcoming them (Barker, 1986).
   - Sensitivity to differences between women, especially those based on social divisions such as class, 'race', age and sexual orientation (Lorde, 1984; Hooks, 1984).
   - Sensitivity to other women's difficulties in expressing themselves and support in overcoming them (Dreifus, 1973).
   - Developing individual women's strength and confidence.
   - Sharing skills and knowledge.
   - Open discussions.
   - Not blaming women for their oppression.
 - Formulating a plan of action:
   - Linking personal experience to the way society structures social relations.
   - Focusing on concrete experiences.
   - Using women's anger constructively.
   - Redefining personal problems as social issues.
   - Focusing on action which can be undertaken to resolve social issues on a collective basis.

Organising Groups

The formation of an active, viable group is an essential element in any campaign. It is vital, therefore, that community activists give considerable thought to the formation of their group and the processes and dynamics on which it operates. The following points are important items requiring consideration and decisions made by those intending to form themselves into a group.

★ *Objectives*
 Clarity of purpose:
 - Why are you setting up a group?
 - What do you expect it to do?
 - Do you understand the problem you are tackling?

* *Group Membership*
  - Who will join the group?
  - How will you get women to join?
  - Are people in the group they think they joined?
  - Is there agreement on the group's aims?
  - Is the group's size compatible with its aims and objectives?
* *Group Name*
  What will you call the group?
  - Depends on your aims and who you are?
  - Difficult to work out.
  - Make it 'catchy' and memorable.
* *Problem Definition*
  - What problem is the group addressing?
  - Who has defined it as the problem?
  - How has the group redefined the problem?
  - Who shares the group's redefinition of the problem?
* *Powers of the Group*
  - What powers does it have?
  - Is the group an advisory one? an independent one? one merely for show?
* *Decision-Making*
  - Is everyone involved in the decision-making processes?
  - Do you wish to have elections to select an executive committee?
  - Are the members of the executive committee accountable to the group?
* *Commitments Expected of Group Members*
  - Time.
  - Money (fees/dues to be included).
  - Practical help (include fund-raising, publicity, organising objectives).

Involving people in practical ways in the group's activities is crucial in maintaining group morale and sustaining the life of the group. These activities should be meaningful to the individuals concerned and should be those to which they commit themselves personally. The group should not coerce people into contributing beyond their willingness to do so (Cook and Kirk, 1983).

* *Group Progress*
  - Progress may be slow. The group will 'gel' as individuals become comfortable with and trust each other.
  - Be clear about the purpose of each meeting.
  - Try to secure an early 'success' in the group's activities to maintain morale (this may be a subsidiary issue which can be dealt with quickly).
  - Decide priorities in the work – these may change over time.

- Have the right atmosphere in the group – be serious, but have fun too.
- Involve all members in the activities of the group.
- Review progress and evaluate the group's action regularly.
- Try to obtain as accurate information for the group as possible.
- Develop the group's 'fact bank' and keep its records up to date.
- Know who the group is trying to influence (decision-makers).
- Decide at what point the group draws other groups into its activities and extends its demands.

★ *Resources*
- What resources does the group have?
- Which resources are internal to the group?
  - Include individual's skills such as research skills, campaigning skills, organising skills, writing/making posters, publicity skills, fund-raising skills, analytical skills (of action and of society).
- Which resources are external to the group?
  - Include premises, personnel resources and material resources such as facilities, equipment and funds, but know what resources the group has already and which it needs to procure.
- What additional resources does the group need to obtain?
- Publicly provided resources from agencies such as local authorities, social services departments, central government. Include premises, funds, and publicity;
- Privately provided resources from charities, trusts, companies, voluntary organisations. Include premises, funds and publicity;
- Material resources such as buildings, stationary, printing and duplicating facilities, films/videos, telephones, office furniture, furnishings; and
- Personnel. People are needed to write publicity and distribute it, hold meetings, organise people and campaigns.
- How will the group get these resources?
- How will the group obtain support from the public?

★ *Action*
- What needs to be done?
- When should it be done?
- How should it be done?
- By whom should it be done?
- Whose attention is the group trying to attract?
- Which decisions is the group trying to change?
- Monitor the group's progress and evalute it.
- Learn from the group's experience.

Chapter 4

Feminist Action in the Workplace

Feminist action in the workplace has sought to highlight the contribution women make to social and economic development both through the waged labour market and their unpaid caring work. It has also revealed the monotony and drudgery which still characterises housework (Oakley, 1974); exposed the damage to women's emotional development and careers caused by the sexual division of labour in both domestic (Gavron, 1966) and waged work (Armstrong, 1984; Coyle and Skinner, 1988); indicated the pervasiveness of sexual harassment in the workplace (Benn and Sedgley, 1984); and identified the compulsion for men to persist in emotionally and physically numbing work in the name of providing for their families (Dominelli, 1986c). In this site too, feminist action has revealed the connections and contradictions between a woman's experience of herself as nurturer in the community and employee in the workplace. Feminists have organised within equal opportunities initiatives to promote egalitarian relations at work, political parties, autonomous feminist groups, and the trade union movement in both male dominated and women-only trade unions. In this chapter we examine feminist action in creating a more conducive working environment and the patchy nature of feminist achievements on this front. I will also show how women's needs as workers can be coterminuous with those of their clients when their nurturing roles are taken into account. These can provide the basis for an empathy resting on shared experiences between women. Additionally, I explore the client-worker relationship and draw parallels between the position of women workers and that of the individuals they serve and consider how the tensions between the care and control side of their work can be tackled from a feminist perspective. Furthermore, this chapter offers suggestions for organisational change aimed at improving women's position in social work and community work.

Unpaid Domestic Work and Low Paid Waged Labour: Women's Lot

Society's definitions of masculinity and femininity are intricately connected to the notion of work. Paid work, particularly its better paid and prestigious elements, belongs to men. Unpaid work in the home is women's lot. This idea pervades the social division of labour, the educational system which prepares people for their roles in society, and the organisation of the family. Feminist scholars have expended considerable energy in exploring the position of women in the labour market and have found that familialist ideology is important in structuring employers' expectations about women employees. Women whose social position is defined by their place in the community are consider temporary incumbents of the workplace. They are expected to leave when they marry or have children. Men are tied to the workplace to meet their responsibility of providing financial support for their families. Hence, waged work for men furnishes a career; for women, it contributes 'pin money' (Coyle and Skinner, 1988).

This definition of work ignores several aspects of reality which are crucial to women's well-being. To begin with, women's lives are constructed around their having one foot at home in the community and the other in the workplace. The one earner two-parent family is not the major family form (Sidel, 1986; Segal, 1987; Eichler, 1983). Two earner couples are necessary for a family to obtain a decent standard of living since neither a man nor a woman working alone can earn a sufficiently high salary to care for a family (Sidel, 1986; Segal, 1987). For single parent families, particularly those headed by women, poverty will be a major obstacle to their acquiring a decent standard of living (Davis, 1989) because even when women work, they earn less than men. Women in Britain, the USA and Canada, for example, earn on average around two-thirds of the male wage (Segal, 1987; Sidel, 1986; Armstrong, 1984). Women tend to work part-time to meet their family responsibilities and are located primarily in the low waged service and retail sectors of the economy. Feminists in Britain and America have campaigned around the issue of women's unequal position in the workplace and demanded equal pay for equal work. In Britain, the Sex Discrimination Act (SDA) was passed in 1970 following feminist social action on this issue. It became effective in 1975 and created an even stricter segregation of labour than existed previously as employers sought to evade its provisions by defining more jobs as 'women only' ones. As a result of their tactics, women's wages which had peaked at 73% of male wages following the implementation of the SDA, have declined to 67% (Segal, 1987). In America, the Equal Economic Opportunities Act was passed in 1964 and was followed by a period of affirmative action. Nonetheless, the position of waged women remains one of lower pay than men and their exclusion from the higher income echelons of the labour hierarchy.

But the waged labour market covers only a fraction of the work women undertake. Women's domestic work in the home, though unpaid makes a substantial contribution to the economy. Yet, this fact is not usually acknowledged in public discussions about work. Domestic work, remains publicly invisible although feminists have brought it into the public arena. An early attempt by feminists to bring domestic labour out into the open was to demand 'wages for housework' (Dalla Costa and James, 1972). The Wages for Housework Campaign has not succeeded in achieving its objective but it has contributed to redefining public understandings of work. One problem with the call for 'wages for housework' was that it was not a demand supported by the feminist movement as a whole. Socialist feminists in particular rejected the specific demand whilst accepting the social importance of work women undertook in the home on the grounds that payment for domestic work would lock women more firmly into the houseworker role. They preferred to see housework socialised and shared equally between men and women. State initiatives in socialising housework in capitalist states have been limited, for example, nursery provision for stigmatised families, and hardly merits being classified as such. China undertook massive socialisation of housework, particularly cooking, laundrying, and childcare during the Great Leap Forward (Andors, 1983). However, the sexist division of labour in the socialised enterprises was maintained. Women performed the bulk of the socialised housework that earned workpoints. Unfortunately, women also performed the bulk of the domestic work that remained to be done in the home. This was not socially recognised as useful work as it did not earn workpoints (Andors, 1983). 'Women's work' continued to be identified as 'women's work' and undervalued whether it was socialised or not. These events suggest that 'men's work' has got to be as much part of a redefinition of labour as 'women's work' if the division of labour is to be transformed into one that does not reinforce sexist divisions.

Feminist initiatives in the workplace have demonstrated a close connection between waged work and unwaged work and shown how one feeds into the other and vice-versa. Much of the work which women do in the waged labour market draws on skills women learn by working in the home. Assuming these are acquired 'naturally' employers make few provisions for training women, thus substantially reducing training costs for waged women. Like housework, women's waged work is devalued and poorly paid. Women also tend to be in subordinate positions, whilst men hold positions commanding authority, power and resources. Moreover, whilst housework has a large element of drudgery (Oakley, 1974), waged work for women can also be tedious, repetitive and monotonous. Inequality at work has made many women prefer to work in the home rather than outside it. For black and working class women, the conditions of paid labour are so awful, that many of them would rather give up their jobs and stay at home if they could afford to exercise this option (Davis, 1989; Hooks, 1984). Waged work may be physically hazardous because women handle dangerous substances, do close work which strains their eyesight and, may be rooted to one spot in uncomfortable positions for lengthy periods, thereby damaging their backs. Feminists have campaigned around health issues in the workplace, transcending traditional approaches to 'health and safety' at work which have focused on wearing protective appareil and restricting access to certain types of work by prioritising preventative health care which enables people to keep their health, for example, cervical screening for women. Such gains may be contradictory for they may intensify pressures to keep women working longer and ignore women's emotional and mental health needs when they are expected to perform a double shift – in waged labour and unpaid domestic work.

Women face additional hazards in waged work which do not confront their male colleagues, for example, sexual harassment which emanates from male workers. Women face physical, psychological and emotional attacks which can destablise their sense of well-being. Feminist action in the workplace has also tackled this issue and made the elimination of sexual harassment an integral part of equal opportunities policies aimed at encouraging women to enter the waged workforce, particularly in traditional male dominated areas, for example, engineering. In defining sexual harassment, feminists have focused on both verbal and physical abuse, demonstrating that its presence creates an atmosphere which intimidates women and prevents them from developing their full potential at work (Benn and Sedgley, 1984; Whittington, 1985). Feminist action on sexual harassment has been fraught with difficulties. Men have resisted acknowledgeing its presence in the workplace and refused to accept responsibility for perpetuating and condoning it. This has meant few men have taken active steps to eradicate it. Feminist initiatives against sexual harassment have also revealed that the problem must be confronted at a number of points, beginning with the socialisation of girls, their work at school, and their training for the world of work. But for feminist efforts on this front to be effective, sexual harassment has to become an issue taken seriously by men. They will have to accept responsibility for their obnoxious behaviour and take determined steps to end it.

Meanwhile, feminists have organised feminist support groups and caucuses to make sexual harassment an issue in the trade union movement and convince employers to adopt policies which make sexual harassment a disciplinary offense. Unions like NAL-GO, NUPE and the AUT have responded to feminist concerns by studying the problem amongst their membership. These have revealed the extensiveness of sexual harassment in women's working life, the reluctance of men to admit its prevalence, the fear which inhibits women from bringing forward complaints, and the difficulties encountered in making sexual harassment a serious workplace issue. Shifting trade union members' and employers' attitudes on this matter has been problematic because it involves men rethinking their attitudes and changing their behaviour in a direction which condemns their previous patterns. Men have to learn that comments, actions, and structures which they had previously accepted as 'normal' have trivialised and degraded women and are socially reprehensible. Whilst agreeing there was a problem, women workers have also been skeptical about the extent to which feminists could successfully challenge such 'natural' male behaviour and introduce new codes of conduct in workplace relations until they saw evidence of men taking the issue seriously. Their response indicates the appropriateness of feminist ways of working which is to encourage women to consider social issues from their own personal position and experience and work through them in their own time.

Making Connections Between Domestic Labour and Waged Labour

Feminists have highlighted the connection between women's work in the home and their access to waged work. They have argued that housework, particularly childcare, should be socialised to free women's time for other activities. Campaigns aimed at improving childcare provisions have featured strongly in feminist social action. This has included campaigns seeking to defend public nursery provisions threatened with closure as part of the public expenditure cuts (e.g. 'Save the Wheatley Street Nursery'), campaigns aimed at ending racist practices in day care centres, (e.g., in Hackney) and campaigns aimed at improving the situation nationally, (e.g. the National Childcare Campaign (NCC)). The majority of struggles around day care for the under-fives are local. Women organise in response to a need – the loss of places, the absence of provisions, the desire to provide children with an anti-sexist and anti-racist environment. Some of these struggles may be protracted, especially if the local authority is being challenged as in the threatened closure of existing facilities. Its response may move women to occupy buildings, as in the case of the 'Save the Wheatley Street Nursery', and undertake all the activities necessary to reach this position. This includes lobbying local councillors, conducting a campaign in the media, working hrough the unions and procuring community support for their position.

Working together, in non-hierarchical ways in such campaigns, women have shared their skills, expertise and fears. Women have sought union support for their cause in unionised workplaces. One way in which unions have taken supportive action has been to facilitate women's access to the buildings they intend to occupy (National Childcare Campaign, 1984). Unions can also furnish useful information and advice on practicalities which need to be followed, provide legal counsel, and negotiate changes in policies with employers. Such collaborative relationships help create links between women in the community and workers, male and female, in the workplace. Women occupying buildings also disrupts family life to a certain extent. Meals will no longer appear on the table. Housework will not get done. Thus, the connection between women having a public role and a private one becomes readily apparent (Cook and Kirk, 1983). Additionally, women draw the community more closely into their action (Gallagher, 1977). This is done by relying on informal networks amongst women to secure political support for them. Women in the community will sign petitions, attend demonstrations and supply those occupying the building with food, drink and bedding. Some women also offer help to members of the family left at home.

Campaigns around childcare issues have been an important aspect of community action. These campaigns have increased in number as nurseries have become casualties of the public expenditure cuts. Many of these campaigns have involved women in a fairly extensive way. Scattered throughout the country, these campaigns were fragmented, replicated other organising efforts and placed those involved in them in the position of learning lessons on strategies and tactics on their own instead of drawing inspiration from other women's struggles (National Childcare Campaign, 1985). This also meant women were unable to offer one another support during moments of acute struggle or demoralisation. However, women from one campaign were spontaneously contacting women involved in other campaigns and meeting them at various conferences and discussion seminars. Women later substantiated these links through mutual support at demonstrations and occupations aimed at saving nurseries. Eventually, these links and contacts were formalised by these women when they launched the NCC in July 1980 (NCC, 1985).

The culmination of women's concern for and support of one another in the formation of the NCC made them and their experience more easily available to other women wishing to protect whatever childcare provisions were available to them. However, some NCC members were not prepared to let the NCC rest at the level of defending their inadequate provisions. They wanted to raise the question of childcare more generally, in terms

91

of women's role in society, their responsibilities vis-a-vis children, and the oppression they experience because of their dual role in waged work and domestic labour.

Many of the specific nursery campaigns handled the problems participants encountered imaginatively, for example, overcoming differences in women's preparedness to undertake 'militant' action, coping with the legal aspects of confrontation between community groups and the authorities, and broadening their base of support. The Wheatley Street Nursery was a case in point.

Women affected by the proposal formed a Parent's Action Group (PAG) to oppose the closure of the Wheatley Street Nursery. At first the PAG organised petitions and lobbies to try and influence the Council's decisions. The group subsequently produced a document which spelt out their reasons for opposing the closure of the nursery. In the meantime, PAG continued meeting with the relevant parties to the dispute. PAG members collectively drew up a series of contigency plans, including the occupation of the building. The right of individual women to determine their own contribution to the struggle was maintained in that no woman in the group was compelled to undertake action to which she personally did not feel committed. PAG also aimed to secure support for their position amongst professionals, trade unionists, and local government employees as well as parents in the community.

These preparations paid off when the building had to be occupied to prevent the nursery from being closed. For example, NUPE endorsed the occupation straightaway. However, under orders from the Council, senior NALGO officials who had not been relating to PAG locked in the women occupying the building. The electricity and gas were also turned off. These actions demonstrate the importance of acquiring support for a campaign at all levels of the trade union before crisis point is reached.

During the occupation of the building, the PAG prepared publicity for the campaign and organised public meetings to present its case and secure support for the occupation. PAG arranged meetings with the local authority officials responsible for the decision to close the nursery and demanded they reverse their decision. It also organised marches to the Council buildings. As they marched through the streets, people sang protest songs PAG members had written. Keeping members actively participating in PAG's activities was one way of keeping up morale and commitment amongst them. In the short-term, their tactics paid off. The occupation was successful and the Wheatley Street Nursery was saved.

The declining birth rate and the lower number of young school-leavers who are reaching the waged labour market at the present time, have caused employers fearing a labour shortage in the near future to rethink their attitudes, policies and provisions regarding women employees (Beynon, 1989). The dwindling supply of young workers coupled with Britain's restrictive position on immigration, means women in the home looking after children and older people form employers largest source of untapped labour. Recognising that they will have to deal with the problem of childcare if they want to attract women into the workforce, private employers are becoming more receptive to feminist demands for adequate childcare provisions, at least for waged working women. In late 1989, some of the larger private companies, for example, the Midland Bank, have provided workplace creches and nurseries so that their employees can be assured of high quality care. Such employers have made these provisions available not because they endorse feminist positions, but because they are aware that such provisions will both attract women workers and have a positive impact on the productivity of those they employ (see Allenspach, 1975). In the public sector, trade unions have also supported feminist demands for nurseries, creches, flexible working hours and job sharing. However, unless discrimination against waged women workers is tackled directly, these measures can be used to further exploit women's labour. Their exploitation is likely to be exacerbated if the resultant increase in productivity is not recognised in the form of pay increases for women, better career prospects for women, the equal involvement of men in childcare work and the creation of egalitarian working relations. In other words, working relations will have to be restructured in keeping with feminist objectives in both the workplace and the home and by abolishing the distinction between 'women's work' and 'men's work'.

Challenging the definition of caring as 'women's work' cannot be limited to childcare. Elder care also needs to be moved out of the female ghetto. Care of older people is already taxing the energies of more women than childcare (Higgins, 1989). Given the demographic makeup of the British population, this work is likely to increase. It is crucial that it is not left as an isolated task women perform in the privacy of their home. Men must be drawn into elder care. Public provisions in this area also need to move in egalitarian directions which do not infantilise older people and increase their dependency. Such provisions will also have to fight against the division of people into the young and the old. Employers will have to direct their attention to the growing numbers of women involved in elder care if they want to meet workforce requirements by attracting women workers. Black people have already established community based provisions which address ageism and racism for their elders (Asian Sheltered Residential Accommodation, 1980).

Alongside their demands for publicly supported childcare (National Childcare Campaign, 1984) and elder care (Doress and Siegal, 1989), feminists have also struggled to secure equal opportunities for women in the workplace. They have worked through their trade unions, joined *ad hoc* equal opportunities committees, formed workplace based support groups and networked with other feminists to introduce equal opportunities policies and practices in waged work. Additionally, sustained feminist and black people's activities on workplace inequalities have compelled public sector unions such as NALGO to establish an Equal Rights Working Party to examine the rights of women, lesbian women, gay men and black people in local government employment. This has come about as a result of these groups organising in autonomous groups within NALGO itself, for example, the Black Members Group. These initiatives have had mixed results. They have raised the public profile of women's inequality at work, opened more sectors of the economy to women workers, made both employers and workers more aware of some of the more blatant forms of discrimination against waged working women, and encouraged employers to monitor recruitment practices, interviewing procedures and promotion opportunities for gender bias (Coyle and Skinner, 1988). However, these moves have not produced the intended results for women. Women who have been recruited to workplaces traditionally dominated by men, are often being forced to leave soon after joining because they encounter so much hostility from male colleagues. Women are subjected to sexist jokes, sexist innuendo and sabotage as men fight to keep them 'in their place' (Beynon, 1989). This picture contrasts sharply with men entering traditionally female occupations, for example, office work, teaching, and nursing. Men are supported by their women colleagues and made to feel comfortable. Their superiors consider them promotion material and they are advanced to the managerial and higher echelons very quickly (Senate Sex Equality Committee, 1986; Beynon, 1989). It seems that equal opportunities policies which focus only on limited aspects of the dynamics leading to gender discrimination at work advance men's interests more readily than they promote equality for women.

Women Workers and Women Clients: Shared Interests

Feminist community workers have sought to establish egalitarian relationships between themselves and the women with whom they work. In redefining the relationship between them, feminist community workers have kept hold of the fact that women in the community may be facing triple workloads – waged work, unwaged housework, and unpaid caring work, and refused to lock women into these categories. Feminist community workers have supported women in making known their plight and raising public consciousness through campaigns, street theatre, audio-visual productions such as films and videos, community newspapers, leaflets, posters, lobbying. At the local level, feminist community workers have attempted to involve men in assuming tasks which are normally considered 'women's work' when attempting to break down the division of labour in the groups they relate to, for example, getting men to mind the children at the creche provided by feminist community groups, supporting women in convincing their partners that they should do the housework and mind the children or care for older relatives to free women wishing to join community groups. And, they have encouraged men in community groups to undertake supportive roles rather than seeking to dominate the group (Curno *et al*, 1982). Encouraging men to support women's involvement in community action in these ways can free both women participating in groups and women community workers from domestic commitments which eat into their time for doing other things.

Whilst acknowledging that they wield power by virtue of their skills as community workers, feminist community workers have tried to reduce it by imparting their knowledge to women they work with and focusing their attention on facilitating women's ability to make their own decisions about the group's orientation and the activities it sponsors. Additionally, they have tried to place women in community groups on a more egalitarian footing with them by developing areas of their shared experiences as women. This has been particularly evident in the redefinition of work so that it includes both waged and unwaged work and assigns significance to both whilst recognising the interdependence that exists between the two spheres. This means for example, that feminist community workers and women in community groups can empathise with the need to establish childcare facilities that suit all their needs and work together as equals to develop these in practice. Demanding facilities that meet the needs of both groups of women mean that they can support each other in arguing for childcare that is available around the clock. Provisions of this nature would open up waged employment opportunities for women and make it easier for them to choose the lifestyles they find most rewarding. Moreover, the concern of both sets of women to provide the best care possible for their children means that they can sit down together to consider what kinds of facilities will also meet their children's needs for intellectual stimulation, emotional fulfillment, physical care, and bodily growth. In other words, they could pool their resources to develop provisions which accorded equal importance to meeting the needs of women waged workers, women working at home and children.

Developing relationships of equality between women community workers and women in the community is crucial if feminist community workers are not going to fall into the trap of enforcing domesticity upon women in the community and arguing that the needs of waged women have priority over those of unwaged women. For if they get caught up in relations of domination and subordination, feminist community workers will be promoting forms of community work which are consistent with social control and reinforce women's domestic role as their lot.

Caring for Older People: Work Undertaken in the Home

Older people constitute a large proportion of the British population. It is estimated that by the 21st century, one-quarter of British people will be aged. Two major problems facing older people today are material poverty and social isolation. A large proportion of older British people is trying to eke out a living on meagre pensions. Because of their low incomes, many older persons are unable to either heat their homes adequately or keep them in a good state of repair. This has meant that many old people die unnecessarily of hypothermia each year and cannot adapt their homes to meet age-related physical needs, for example, having easy access to bathrooms, bedrooms and central heating.

The debilitating effects of poverty during old age are most likely to be experienced by women. Women constitute the largest proportion of the older age group. They are also the ones who have the lowest incomes. Townsend discovered that older women were likely to have half the income of older men at their disposal (Townsend, 1979).

The social isolation of older people cannot automatically be attributed to increased frailty generated by declining physical health due to old age (Doress and Siegal, 1988). Rather, it has to be understood in terms of ageism – or discrimination against older people on the basis of their age and the devaluation of their contribution to society as carers of others and retired waged workers. In British society, once people lose their productive role in both the waged and unwaged work arenas, they lose their place in society (Phillipson, 1982). This loss of status and role causes individuals to experience loss of confidence, low self-esteem and a feeling of uselessness and irrelevance to others. These feelings are major threads running through the lives of older people living on low incomes. Consequently, older people are made to feel powerless and overwhelmed by the mere fact of their existence. Such feelings are particularly oppressive for older women whose experience of ageing is more problematic than men's because they have lost social significance as beings with a purpose and are denied their sexuality. Additionally, the experience of ageism is different for women than for men because women face ageism at a younger age, are more likely than men to live out old age in poverty, are stigmatised to a greater degree and endure more isolation (Doress and Siegal, 1988). Ultimately, to eliminate ageism, the basis on which society is organised must be changed in accordance with feminist principles. According to these, people secure dignity and purpose by virtue of their being alive and not by the productive role they occupy in society. In the interim, however, older women are beginning to react against the treatment being meted out to them and organise themselves as carers and pensioners.

The working relations of women caring for adult dependents in the home are indicative of women's subordinate position in society. Unpaid carers working from home are unsupported and isolated. The burden of caring for dependent adults falls largely on women who can be caring for children and holding waged employment at the same time (Bonny, 1984). Women who are compelled to give up paid work and any independent life of their own can find their predicament extremely distressing. Single women are often expected to volunteer their care so that their married sisters can be spared. This places them in the unenviable position of having their welfare subordinated to their siblings who are servicing men. The pitting of a single woman's welfare against her married sister's is not only an unequal one in which the social balance is heavily tipped against the unwed woman, it also damages her emotional well-being and distorts her relationships with her sisters if she harbours resentment at being landed with the task. Her brothers are not called upon to make similar sacrifices.

Whilst the position of unpaid carers in the home is appalling, the state is increasing its demands for their labour by closing institutional provisions as part of its public expenditure cuts. Ageism has left older people unprotected and has had a major impact in limiting welfare provisions for older women. Poverty in old age, the product of low incomes in women's unwaged and low waged work, makes it virtually impossible for women (especially working class and black women) to buy private pensions to ease the hardships of old age. They are reliant on miserly state provisions and the support they can obtain from family and friends (Stack, 1975). This means that older women will often be cared for by other women either 'in the community' meaning theirs or their daughter's (in-law) home with little public support, or in private or public nursing homes. Women constitute 71% of kinship based carers (Older Women's League, 1986) and the bulk of the workforce providing caring in both state and private market provisions. The appalling lack of socially provided support to carers of older people has prompted feminists to develop support networks. These are a source of support to individual caregivers and aim to challenge society's neglect of older people and its ageist practices in both the home based and institutional care that is offered. In Britain, the National Association of Carers links up local carers support groups and presses for legislative changes and improved services for carers, those they care for and their families.

In the USA, the Grey Panthers and the Older Women's League amongst others, pull together local support groups. Feminists have established carers' support groups to question society's neglect of the needs of women caring for older people (Bonny, 1984) and in the course of doing so challenge ageism, or the oppression people experience when they get old. Their concerns straddle the needs of both the carer and those being cared for.

Organising Around Old Age

Carers' support groups provide a supportive environment in which carers can discuss their problems openly, sharing with others their experiences and frustrations of giving care to dependent adults. By sharing their concerns, carers discover that they are not alone in facing the problems that make their task unenviable. Consciousness-raising is an important dimension in carers' support groups. It not only develops women's understanding of the relationship between their personal situation as unsupported carers who have to keep sacrificing their own wishes and needs to provide the care they do because society has neglected their needs, but it also enables women to comprehend more fully the nature of the resources that are available and initiate the development of more appropriate services for carers and those they care for. There is a debate about the most appropriate forms of care for older people – institutional or family based care that is consistent with feminist principles (see Finch, 1984; Dominelli, 1981). The position is a tricky one to resolve in that to be consistent with feminist principles, neither the interests of the carer nor the person they are caring for can be subordinated to the other's. This means that institutional care may be appropriate for some people provided that both the caring relations and the working relations in such institutions follow feminist theory and practice. This means having institutions which are collectively run on egalitarian lines, involve both careworkers and the people they are caring for in the decision-making processes, ensure residents lead as independent a life as is compatible with their mental and physical capacities and right to control their destiny, and live a full life in which all their human and civil rights are respected including the right to invite long-term visitors to 'their home', have privacy and undertake sexual activity. Carers support groups also enable members to share knowledge about resources available to them, learn about health problems in old age, bring in specialist speakers, and organise social and fund-raising activities.

Organising around old age has been undertaken by both carers and older people themselves. They have formed feminist campaigns and networks, for example, the Grey Panthers started by Maggie Kuhn in the USA, the Older Women's League (Doress and Siegal, 1987). These organisations have begun unravelling ageist stereotypes by:

★ Challenging ageism and society's definition of old age, especially its enforced dependency, symbolised in compulsory retirement ages;
★ Redefining the 'elderly' as older people or elders in recognition of their experience in life and wisdom, again challenging ageist assumptions of their position;
★ Highlighting the connection between women's low incomes in old age and their position of enforced economic dependency on men in the marriage relationship, interrupted working careers to care for others – children, aged relatives and aged husbands, and low wages when in waged work;
★ Breaking down barriers between different age groups and challenging the division of people into young and old;
★ Demonstrating the strengths of older women and building up their sense of pride and confidence;
★ Identifying the specific health needs of older women in non-ageist terms;
★ Giving older women their voice.

Areas which have been identified as problematic by older people themselves include:

★ Ageist definitions of their position.
★ Their feelings of isolation.
★ Their wish to remain independent and in their own homes.
★ Their dependency on their relatives and children to visit and provide them with social contacts.
★ Low incomes/low pensions.
★ Poor transportation. Taxis are expensive. Buses are difficult to manage and sometimes expensive as well.
★ Bad housing.
★ Good housing, but inadequate for their current needs, especially regarding size and facilities available.
★ The inadequacy of domicillary services, especially lack of home helps, meals-on-wheels, gardeners.
★ A complicated social services system.
★ The lack of centres for older people and open spaces which are easily accessible to them.
★ A monitoring service to check on their safety.
★ The high price of fuel and other necessities of life.
★ The absence of a service which helps people prepare for an active post-retirement life.
★ Inadequate and expensive communications systems for older people.
★ The expense and poor availability of aids and adpatations.

Community workers in Britain have paid scant attention to the needs of older people and have until recently not been involved in direct work with them. This is changing, however, as older people are taking the initiative in organising themselves. Recently, the British Pensioners and Trade Unions Action Association (BPTUAA) has been extremely active in organising older people locally and nationally. It operates as a mixed organisation catering for the needs of both older men and women. Older people involved in BPTUAA have arranged conferences, drawn up their manifesto of demands, and organised demonstrations against government policy on low pensions and high fuel charges which burden older people. Although the organisation's activities can be criticised for not making radical demands which challenge institutionalised ageism in society in the way that their American feminist counterparts have done, its impact in organising older people, and affecting the consciousness of British pensioners and their perceptions of their rights and entitlements should not be minimised. Neither should we ignore BPTUAA's effect on the trade union movement by making some trade unions recognise that older people are part of the working-class whose interests should form an integral part of their concerns and responsibilities. The organisation's paper, the *British Pensioner*, is a major undertaking aimed at improving communications between pensioners as well as letting others know which areas of life are most problematic for them. It is possible for community activists to become involved in organising with older people through such organisations. However, they should make sure that they see their role very much in a servicing capacity, or as facilitators in a process in which older people make the demands and control the show.

BPTUAA's demands, as expressed in their declaration of intent, are wide ranging and attempt to cover most aspects of need affecting pensioners. Besides demanding their dignity, independence and security as full members of society, they cover income, housing, the personal social services, fuel allowances, health care, education and recreational facilities, inflation-linked pensions, tax-free Christmas bonuses, the retention of their pension if they work after retirement and a death grant. Feminists' task is to respond positively to these demands.

'We're All In It Together' – Women Against Pit Closures

Feminist community action has consistently argued that workplace relations and domestic arrangements are intricately linked. The protracted British miners strike of 1984–5 provided an example of community action which linked community issues with workplace issues and involved alliances covering a cross-section of the population locally and nationally. Women Against Pit Closures initially defended their mining communities as these were threatened with decimation if the pits closed. But, in the course of their struggle, women developed both their gender consciousness and class consciousness. Women refused to remain on the sidelines in a subordinate role to men. Protecting their communities meant women had to leave them and try to convince others to support their cause. Women travelled the length and breadth of the country giving talks, appearing on television and performing their own sketches of the situation. To be free to undertake public activities of this nature, domestic arrangements had to be changed, for the domestic division of labour by which women were responsible for the housework acted as a drag on their involvement. These were challenged, and men used to going home to their wives' cooked meals began cooking for them instead. In some communities, domestic tasks, for example, cooking and childcare, were also socialised to enable individual mining communities to survive lengthy conflict and stretch limited financial resources. Women remained primarily responsible for collective welfare services, but whilst working in them, women talked to each other about their experience and developed a sense of solidarity and awareness of their position as *working class women.* The classist and gendered nature of society became very visible to them. As did the repressive might of the state, including the way in which it spent millions on policing their communities but was unable to finance better health care and other welfare services.

Acquiring these social insights prompted women to ask questions about the way in which society was organised and for whose benefit things were as they were. Their greater awareness also drew women closer together and enabled women from mining communities to take major roles in forming alliances with different groups of women – academic women, lesbian women, black women, white women. These groups of women also supported women from mining communities in their struggles in practical ways – financially and by demonstrating and signing petitions. Although the Women Against Pit Closures and National Union of Minworkers (NUM) were unable to prevent the closure of a number of mines, the experience profoundly changed relationships between some men and women in mining communities and raised questions about the kind of life people wanted to lead (MCrindle and Rowbotham, 1986; Lewycka, 1986). The realisation that men and women were needed to fight for their communities and that what happened at work had serious repercussions for home life and affected women and children as well as men led Women Against Pit Closures to request associate membership in the NUM so that they could influence its policies. However, this proposal was rejected by the NUM as many men felt threatened by the power that feminists could potentially acquire if women joined the union in this capacity.

Feminist Prefigurative Forms

Besides these activities which indicate feminist action in penetratring existing provisions and changing them, feminists have created a variety of autonomous feminist ventures which endorse feminist principles and practice in the workplace. These prefigure the non-oppressive social relations feminist aim to establish in society as a whole. These efforts have covered a range of autonomous initiatives in the community and have included restructured traditional workplaces, for example, the Lee Jeans Cooperative, commercial unwaged cooperatives such as food cooperatives on council housing estates, commercial wages cooperatives such as the *Spare Rib* collective, feminist services located within the public sector such as the Well-Women Clinics within the NHS, voluntary organisations which include carers' support groups, rape crisis centres, incest survivor lines, women's refuges, women's resources centres and women's therapy centres. These initiatives have enabled women to challenge definitions of work, workplaces and working relations. Women working together collectively is one of their major thrusts. Women working in them have begun to reduce hierarchical relations in all their manifestations by tackling a variety of social divisions including class, 'race', gender, disability and social orientation, reducing differentials in pay, status and skills, eliminating the division between the managers and those being managed, blurring the distinctions in work processes between workers and users; involving both waged workers and consumers in the decision-making processes of the enterprise, acknowledging the interconnections between the demands of home-life and waged working life and giving women's interests a high profile in their activities.

The British Well-Women Clinics (WWCs) are illustrative of feminist prefigurative working relations (Deacon, 1983; Foster, 1989; Doyal, 1983). As such, they represent feminist workplaces carved out within the interstices of paid work and unpaid self-help work in which service providers undertake to work with service users collectively and democratically in ways that address directly those points at which their interests are at variance with each other's. Feminists have formed WWCs both outside and inside the NHS, depending on the extent of local support or hostility generated when putting forward proposals to provide women-centered and controlled spaces and health care. Eschewing the passive patient role and its emphasis on curative medicine, WWCs have aimed to provide health care which is more responsive to women's needs. They have been founded on the belief that women have a right to participate actively in their health care, and have fostered preventative approaches to medical care. WWCs teams are composed of doctors, nurses, and volunteers seeking to work together in less hierarchical ways. This enables WWC workers to learn medical, organisational and interpersonal skills from each other. Their efforts are not always successful as users may respond to volunteer's advice with less alacrity than a doctor's, thereby devaluing volunteers' experience and status (Foster, 1989). Besides fostering more equitable relationships, this approach also maximises the use of available resources. In these ways, WWCs offer alternative working relations to the problematic ones encountered by feminists working individually within NHS hospital settings. Working on their own, they may become isolated and extremely vulnerable as Wendy Savage discovered (Savage and Leighton, 1986).

By adopting a holistic approach to medical care, WWCs give women sufficient time to talk through their concerns so that both their physcial and emotional states are considered in the treatment. Professionals working within them work with each woman as a complete person whose interdepenent parts make up the whole individual. Listening is also important in validating women's own definition of their health needs. Preventative strategies and listening strategies have freed WWCs from relying on drugs and surgery in dealing with women's health problems. Moving away from drugs also facilitates the process whereby women can play a more active role in their treatment programme. Workers in WWCs are expected to be sensitive, caring, and show their own vulnerability and emotions throughout their interaction with the women seeking treatment. By these means, WWCs challenge the neutral, uninvolved professionalism of traditional approaches and begin the task of redefining the professional role. Working in this way carries dangers for the practitioners if they do not take care of themselves. They may find they become totally exhausted. Foster (1989) reports one WWC which closed down after two years because of worker 'burn out'.

WWCs aim to dissolve social divisions and reach women who do not normally use medical facilities. However, inadequate resources have impeded progress on this front. The numbers of working class and black women using these facilities are limited. WWCs have sought to tackle this problem by seeking urban aid funding (Foster, 1989). Such funding is limited and precarious. Outstanding amounts of grants can be suddenly and unilaterally withdrawn. Funding is also dependent on women acquiring the support of both local and central states. Receiving approval can be difficult for projects deemed to have 'political aims'. Additionally, workers appointed through urban aid are marginalised as they do not enter the career structures of mainstream health services. The employment of black women under such terms endorses institutionalised racism. WWCs are themselves marginal provisions, whether inside or outside the NHS. Their marginalisation limits their potential to control employment policy and practice in the wider NHS, but they can be part of a struggle aimed at eradicating racism and ensuring that black women are given access to promotions within the NHS.

Although one hundred area health authorities had WWCs in 1987 (Foster, 1989:345), the name has been misued by some authorities which have included family planning clinics in this classification simply because they are staffed by women. These do not practice according to feminist principles (Foster, 1989). WWCs often operate on a shoe-string. For example, the first WWC to open in Manchester provided one clinic session per week. Others have restricted hours, further limiting their accessibility to women. WWCs located within GPs' surgeries do not receive state funding for services other than cervical smears made available to women aged over 35 once every three to five years (Foster, 1989).

WWCs have strengths and weaknesses defined by their being self-help initiatives carved out of a dominant medical model antagonistic to their existence. Their provisions are easily accessible because they are located in the community they are intended to serve. The practitioners within them exercise a degree of autonomy in running their affairs. But, their size means that the workers' time and energies are consumed by the activities of keeping the WWC going (Foster, 1989). This leaves little time for either further developmental or outreach work. Limited resourcing also means that only small numbers of women can receive the services WWC provide. Waiting lists for feminist health provisions can be lengthy too (McLeod, 1987). Their service is also hindered by their being unable to act as referral centres to other NHS resources. WWCs can be abused by unsupportive NHS doctors who will pass 'difficult' women on to them (Foster, 1989). WWCs are therefore, unlikely to threaten established medical interests in the NHS. But on the positive side, WWCs offer women services not otherwise available, increase the choice of women in the community, and provide women with a treatment they can en-thuse over (Foster, 1989).

WWCs have had a limited impact on the dominant mode of service delivery and labour organisation in the NHS. Their significance is more local, including giving women more choices about where to go for medical attention. They stand as examples of good medical practice that does not rely on the glorification of high technology medicine which makes patients feel powerless and alienated (Doyal, 1986).

The presence of feminist self-help provisions should make the market more responsive to women's needs. In practice, at least in the USA, feminists have discovered that the contrary holds. Medical service providers, especially large health care corporations have cynically used the information gathered through feminist ventures to provide more high technology medicine and drug oriented therapies for women, for example, progesterone therapy in treating the Pre-Menstrual Syndrome. They have also attracted healthy women to use their facilities by promising them more fulfilling lives; and cater to women in the higher income brackets (Dreifus, 1973; Ruzek, 1986; Worcester and Whatley, 1988). The scenario in Britain depends largely on whether the Tories dismantle the NHS or whether more consumer oriented democratic reforms take place. If the opposition to Tory proposals to dismember the NHS prevents it happening, reforms in keeping with the latter possibility might occur. These could take the form of curbing doctors powers, making them salaried state employees instead of independent contractors and giving consumers a greater voice in the NHS' power structures and administration (Iliffe, 1985). Simply having doctors become state workers will not guarantee the empowerment of consumers. The present welfare state stands as witness to how far removed from clients expectations the services provided by state employees can be (Croft and Beresford, 1986). Employment in state welfare can make workers less rather than more sensitive and produce more bureaucratic, remote and alienating provisions (Maynard and Bosanquet, 1986). In the final analysis, change conducive to people's welfare will only take place if either the ruling elite promotes it in this direction, or grassroots activity can force its rulers to act in those terms. Changes giving women equality will not endure if they are not underwritten by the infusion of feminist principles in theory and practice at both central and local state levels and in society more generally (Dominelli and McLeod, 1989).

Chapter 5
Feminist Political Action

Feminist intervention in the political sphere has been guided by the realisation that 'the personal is political' (Dreifus, 1973), 'the political is personal' (Ungerson, 1987) and 'sisterhood is universal' (Adamson *et al*, 1988) and has led to a redefinition of 'politics'. That is, feminists have rejected definitions of politics which focus only on the electoral process and exclude women. The casting of one's votes every four or five years couples the abrogation of one's responsibilities as a citizen to a remote and rarely accountable (usually male) elected representative with an action which demystifies the gendered nature of power in all social interaction, places power in women's hands and combines personal responsibility with collective accountability. All feminist social action is political because it is concerned with dissolving power relations that establish hierarchies between people and transforming society at all levels – political, social, economic, cultural and personal. Amongst other things, meeting this objective entails changing the relations that exist between men and women, between adults and children, and between women and both local and central states. Feminists have therefore engaged in the political processes of government and sought to place feminist social action on their agendas. Feminists' understandings of political processes transcends the definition of politics that concerns itself primarily with the party political arena. Feminist politics seek to eliminate the separation of politics into the public realm of electoral politics, which people influence by casting their vote, and all other decisions which profoundly affect people's lives but which are made, on their behalf, by elected representatives (Dominelli and Jonsdottir, 1988).

Feminist political action in Britain has centred around the activities of women's committees sponsored by the local state, particularly in London (Tobin, 1990; Campbell *et al*, 1986; Whitlock, 1987). The cutbacks in their remit or their abolition in certain authorities, have highlighted the vulnerability of feminist community action that is not buttressed by the central state and the support of the population at large. In other countries, for example, Iceland, feminist political parties intervening in the electoral process have been established (Dominelli and Jonsdottir,

1988). Neither of these paths to power have resulted in feminist principles and practice becoming significant aspects of local and central states. Nevertheless, their development has demonstrated that without feminist action in both these levels and the integration of feminist action vis-a-vis the state with other feminist initiatives in the community, there is scant opportunity for the transformation of social relations in accordance with feminist ojbectives. For many of the provisions feminists have demanded require substantial inputs from public funds and changes in the social distribution and use of power and resources. The lessons to be learnt from unsuccessful examples of feminist political action will be identified in this chapter and the case made for ensuring that feminist political action permeates both local and central state structures.

Feminism and Municipal Socialism

Feminist political action has taken place through a variety of forms ranging from women's sections in existing major political parties to the formation of a Women's Party concerned with getting women the vote as in the USA at the turn of the century (Irwin, 1971) and a feminist party attempting to challenge patriarchal representative democracy, as in the case of Kwenna Frambothid in Iceland in the 1980s (Dominelli and Jonsdottir, 1989). British feminists have worked to secure change through existing political parties and the labour movement. Their most recent innovative efforts have occurred through Labour controlled local authorities attempting to practice 'municipal socialism' which has included eliminating 'race' and gender oppression as an essential element in socialist praxis (Livingstone, 1987). These local authorities were located primarily in some of the larger cities, for example, Leeds, Sheffield, Birmingham, Bradford. Some now defunct metropolitan counties and the Greater London Council (GLC) established either Women's Committees for Women's Equal Opportunities Officers to promote women's welfare or appointed leading feminists as staff, for example, Valerie Amos in the Camden Borough Council's Women's Committee, Hilary Wainwright in the GLC's Women's Unit and Lee Comer in Bradford's Women Committee. The demise of the metropolitan and GLC levels of government through their abolition by the Thatcher government indicates the importance of having a feminist political presence in the national state and brings home the vulnerability of feminist initatives that are located in the margins of local state activity. The marginalising of feminist political action subordinates their work to electoral vicissitudes. Labour authorities retaining electoral popularity have continued supporting these initiatives, for example, Leeds and Manchester. Others which found their electoral bouyancy punctured panicked into scapegoating feminists and left activists. An example of this was the axing of the Birmingham Women's Committee when Labour's share of the vote declined during the 1987 local elections (Whitlock, 1987). Attacks on feminist initiatives during moments of electoral adversity has seriously damaged feminist gains regarding equal opportunities policies, childcare programmes, women's safety, women's health and research projects on women's needs (Armstrong, 1987).

The Women's Committee Support Unit of the GLC, the Camden Council's Women's Unit, the Birmingham Council Women's Unit, Sheffield's Equal Opportunities Officer for Women and Leeds' Equal Opportunities Officer for Women provide major examples of feminist ventures within the local state. In these, women workers have made furthering the interests of women as both workers and users of services their main objectives. Such initiatives have recognised that women face specific problems which men do not and have given priority to addressing them by establishing links with women in the community. Women normally excluded from local authority provisions were given particular attention. These included lesbian women, disabled women, older women and black women. Reaching women in novel ways and involving them in the decision-making processes of the local authority constituted major elements of their agenda. As feminist councillors had played key roles in promoting the development of Women's Units and often had them included in their portfolios, Units could draw on existing feminists networks to facilitate their work of reaching women normally ignored by local authorities. Working groups were one strategy adopted by feminists to make links between councillors and women in the community. These working groups held open meetings through which local women residents could participate in moving local state power downwards and outwards. The establishment of community forums was another venue through which this purpose was facilitated. In Camden, for example, the Women's Unit created women's forums through which women residents met directly with women councillors. However, these arrangements were flawed. The working groups and forums lacked power in that they could only make recommendations to the full council if the women councillors accepted the often controversial and radical demands being made. Local women were disadvantaged in having to rely on personalities to convey their wishes, thereby subverting feminist commitments to participative democracy. They were also unable to challenge either political priorities or the hierarchical nature of the political decision-making process which itself marginalised women, as the woman councillor heading the Women's Unit in Birmingham discovered when she was sacked for allegedly jeopardising Labour's electoral prospects by promoting women's equality (Whitlock, 1987).

Additionally, the Women's Unit activities were poorly funded. For example, in 1984, the GLC allocated £500,000 for *all* the city-wide initiatives launched by its Women's Unit, moreover, this funding was vulnerable. Authorised under Section 137 of the 1972 Local Government Act, its existence depended on the willingness of central government to continue it. The anti-feminist and anti-socialist sentiments of the Thatcher government in charge of funding were echoed at the local level by its supporters who condemned the use of Section 137 monies for either feminist or socialist purposes.

The success of these Units to reach groups formerly disenfranchised in local authority provisions contributed to their undoing. The radical nature of some of the demands which women in the community made of the Women's Units, for example, the provision of hostels and refuges for prostitutes working the Kings Cross area of London and transport for lesbian women, were used by the popular press and the Conservative opposition to accuse Labour of being under the control of the 'looney left' and mishandling public money by serving the interests of 'unworthy and unrepresentative' groups such as lesbians, prostitutes and gay men. Their views found resonance amongst right-wing Labour councillors who had been uneasily supporting their more progressive colleagues (*News on Sunday*, 1987:13). Homophobic, racist and sexist opposition to these ventures ensured that many of the activities sponsored by the Women's Unit ceased when the abolition of the GLC terminated their funding. That such sentiments should prevail in public bodies charged with promoting the welfare of *all* residents in their locality serves to highlight how much more work feminists need to undertake, if their theory and practice is to infuse local government structures. It also demonstrates how important it is to have feminist gains underwritten at all levels of society if they are to be protected from attack. (This includes the trade union movement, community groups, political parties and the local and central state.)

An Autonomous Feminist Political Organisation: Lessons from Iceland

Feminists in Iceland have attempted to influence the electoral process in dramatic ways by establishing a feminist political party, Kwenna Frambothid (KF) in November 1981. Entering the arena as a new force, KF women organised themselves according to egalitarian principles. Their Party programme was developed collectively. All women in the Party had a role in promoting it amongst the electorate. Women supported each other in learning how to handle the media by role-playing their parts with each

109

other, and sharing their skills and experiences so that they could learn from one another. They attracted a sizeable share of the vote under a system of proportional representation and successfully elected feminist councillors in Reykjavik and Akureyri, the two largest cities in the 1982 local elections. KF councillors maintained links with the feminist movement outside of the local state by networking and holding open meetings to enable women in the community to have direct access to them, develop an understanding of the issues that women in the community were concerned about, facilitate feminist research, support the creation of specific resources for women such as a women's resource centre, a women's newspaper, a refuge, and attract working class women (Dominelli and Jonsdottir, 1988).

The formation of the Organisation of Women in the Labour Market (SKV) was a major initiative aimed at recruiting working class women and providing them with an organisation tackling inequality in the workplace. Additionally, KF supported women in direct action as they attempted to raise public consciousness about women's plight. The format adopted in raising consciousness was often highly imaginative. For example, KF women protested women's low wages by staging a public demonstration in Reykjavik's supermarkets. Selecting the ingredients for rice pudding which a male government minister had promoted as being nutritious and within the financial reach of all Icelanders, the demonstrating women offered to pay 60% of the price of the goods since women earned that proportion of men's wages. Some of the perplexed women cashiers accepted the amounts tendered, others called their male managers. When KF women refused to leave and started singing protest songs and dancing in the supermarkets, the managers called the police(men). The police helplessly watched the women's performance, trying to tread a fine line between maintaining law and order and allowing a peaceful protest. The women protesters left the premises of their own accord once they had made their point. Their protest made interesting copy in the newspapers.

The KF women's organisational daring also came to the fore when they responded to a sexist challenge inadvertently pronounced by Reykjavik's major at a 'beauty contest'. He commented that if KF women had such beauties amongst their supporters, they would have no problem in ensuring women's equality in the council chambers. KF women arranged to bring their 'beauty contest' protest into Reykjavik Council's deliberations. Assuming the titles of virtues men wish women to hold (for example, 'Miss Patience') the KF women entered the meeting room. One KF councillor (the other one refused to participate in the proceedings) read out a statement from the group and tabled their comments on each Agenda item. The group then sat down and said nothing further for the rest of the meeting. The media which had been alerted to the action had a field day, much to the discomfiture of the mayor (Dominelli and Jonsdottir, 1988).

For a brief period, KF women's commitment, the newness of the venture and the enthusiasm of women participants worked, giving Icelandic women a sense of power in the electoral arena and reducing hierarchies between the elected representatives and women residents. However, the hierarchical structures, within which the feminist councillors had to operate, quickly sapped KF's organisational initiatives and distorted the processes and group dynamics they had established between themselves and the women electorate. Considering the councillors' response to lengthy council agendas destroyed the spontaneity of the meetings councillors held with their constituents and prevented them from raising other issues which were of concern to them. Demoralisation and disillusionment set in, creating divisions amongst the women (Dominelli and Jonsdottir, 1988). The failure of KF to tackle key impediments to women's full involvement in political activities contributed to their disenchantment. KF lacked a position on the role of men in the organisation, failed to tackle inequality arising from women's responsibilities in the home as well as waged work. Also, by responding to issues on an *ad hoc* basis, KF did not offer women a vision of the future. The failure of KF women to agree on their approach to electoral politics caused a split between feminist women and woman-centered women. The latter went on to form Kwenna Listin (KL) whilst KF folded up. The basis of their disagreement was critical to feminist strategies in the electoral arena. KF women who refused to join KL felt that their experience of the electoral process warranted their removing themselves from it to serve women's interests more effectively as an autonomous organisation outside of state political processes. KL women felt that the modest gains they had made in improving women's welfare, raising women's issues for debate and extending women's involvement in traditional parties, demanded their continued participation in electoral structures. They felt there had been a shift leftwards as the other major political parties adopted women candidates and gave women's issues a higher profile to offset erosion in support from progressive factions. KL women stood for the 1983 and 1986 national elections and won a number of seats (Dominelli and Jonsdottir, 1988).

The Icelandic experience suggests that the formation of a feminist political party alone cannot transform the electoral process and orient it in feminist directions. Rather, its existence in isolation from a feminist presence at all levels of society is likely to dissipate feminists energies and lead to the fracture that occurred (Dominelli and McLeod, 1989). Moreover, the price feminists may have to pay for becoming involved in the electoral process in the short-term is the negatation of feminist egalitarian principles.

Feminist Political Action Outside Electoral Politics

Existing political institutions have proven poor vehicles for promoting feminist aims and objectives. British feminists have attempted to transcend the limitations involved in these by developing forums which could unite the different groupings in the progressive left, 'fragments' as they came to be called (Rowbotham *et al*, 1979). The 'Beyond the Fragments Conference' was the first of these initiatives. Socialists disillusioned with the Labour Party followed this with conferences which have still failed to 'unite the fragments' in effective opposition to Thatcherism. Other initiatives by feminists have focused on changing their personal politics and have given rise to 'identity politics' which enable them to change particular forms of oppression affecting them personally (Adams, 1989). The danger of this strategy is that it will fragment feminist initiatives even further, and ignore the broader sources of oppression emanating from social divisions other than gender, for example 'race', class and disability (Hooks, 1984). However, it is important to recognise that feminists need to work towards unity with women whose experience of oppression is unlike theirs:

> 'our different experiences often meant that we had different needs, that there was no one strategy or formula for the development of political consciousness. By mapping out various strategies, we affirmed our diversity while working towards solidarity (Hooks, 1984:58).

Additionally, feminists have undertaken a range of women-only initiatives which challenge both the lack of provisions aimed at meeting women's specific needs and total orientation of late capitalist society. The women's peace movement is illustrative of these. It has uncovered connections between the squandering of social resources on armaments whilst children around the world die of hunger; the massive profits made by multinational companies dealing in weapons; the failure of these corporations to pay taxes; the destruction of non-military jobs to provide resources to the defence industry and the usurping of welfare monies to feed the war machine (Davis, 1989). Feminists have redefined the concept of defence by arguing for nonviolent solutions to social conflict. An examination of the implications of the Greenham Common Women's Peace Movement for feminist community action follows.

The Greenham Common Women's Contribution to Feminist Political Action

The women's peace camp at Greenham Common, unlike its mixed counterparts, the Campaign for Nuclear Disarmament (CND) and European Nuclear Disarmament Campaign (END) and its local derivatives, (e.g. the Leamington European Nuclear Disarmament Campaign – LEND) is a women-only endeavour based on feminist principles. Its feminist stance has separated Greenham Common from other initiatives women have mounted for peace, for instance, Olga Maitland's Families for Peace. Maitland's group supports the multilateral disarmament position advocated by the British government. Greenham embodies a different kind of politics which links people's welfare, world peace and local forms of organisation in empowering those whose normal experience is one of powerlessness. Its commitment to change is total, demanding the radical alteration of intimate personal relations and more remote social ones. Its organising potential depends on the creative use of limited resources which people bring with them when confronting a powerful state backed by multinational finance. This form of organisation has drawn its strength from its readiness to facilitate individual contributions to the collective effort according to their own personal assessment of it (Dominelli, 1986b).

This principle has enabled Greenham Women to maintain loyalty to the group, interact with each other on a more egalitarian basis and, be absolved from feeling guilty for not conforming to group expectations. These organisational advantages have been engendered by its commitment to feminist principles of practice. Unlike traditional groups which rely on group coercion to force individuals to commit themselves beyond their personal capacity for commitment and engender feelings of guilt if they fail to respond in prescribed ways, Greenham Women's responsibility to the group was discharged by each individual woman admitting where her personal limits lay (Cook and Kirk, 1983).

The Greenham Common Women's Peace Movement was created spontaneously by a group of women who had not previously participated in political activities. Women formed the Camp after marching from Cardiff to Greenham in August 1981 to protest the siting of Cruise missiles in Britain. Their major motivation was the nightmarish one of seeing powerful military figures, over whom they had no control, threaten to plunge the world into a nuclear holocaust thereby holding to ransom their own and others lives and threatening to destroy the planet (Cook and Kirk, 1983). Fear for the future fired their determination to resist the escalation of nuclear weaponry by taking direct community based political action and demanding British unilateral nuclear disarmament. These women organised without the aid of community workers. Belying their assumed powerlessness as women, they demonstrated women have power which they can exercise in novel ways.

The Greenham Women created a peace camp which ultimately became a women-only one capable of surviving continuous harassment – threats of eviction, imprisonment and state violence. Greenham women formed a women-only camp after considerable discussion amongst themselves. Not all the women were adherents of feminist theory and practice, but their experience during the brief period in which the camp was a mixed one prompted them to exclude men from their activities. During their sojourn at Greenham, men supporters established patriarchal forms of organisation. These included hierarchical relationships amongst participants; the control of knowledge and organisational skills by a small clique; men occupying the key decision-making roles; aggressive stances towards others; the endorsement of violence and the sexual harassment of women (Cook and Kirk, 1983).

Eschewing patriarchal forms of organising, the women at Greenham resisted the exclusion of women from the public arena. They held machismo responsible for pushing the world to the brink of nuclear war and rejected all it stood for. Maintaining that only women could deconstruct male forms of organisation, they set up a women-only camp and developed new ways of structuring social relations amongst themselves. The presence of feminists at Greenham meant that there was an ideology which countered patriarchy and offered women an alternative world view (Feminism and Non-Violence Study Group, 1983). It also provided a constituency outside the Base through the Women's Liberation Movement from which Greenham women could draw support.

Greenham women's decision to have a women-only camp enabled them to increase their contact with other women and discover how women could work collaboratively with one another. Working collectively together enabled women to focus on eroding the social divisions which existed amongst them, particularly those concerning class, 'race', disability, age and homophobia. And it enabled them to confront familial ideology and the constraints it placed on women's ability to participate in public activities and events, highlight in another arena the link between women's place in the home and their involvement in public life. Greenham women experienced the pain of leaving their families, particularly their children, but they discovered that they, their children and their partners could cope. Many of their menfolk were compelled to accept 'women's work' as their own, thereby challenging their own stereotypes and attitudes (Cook and Kirk, 1983).

Men feared the power of women symbolised by the Greenham women. They felt threatened by their exclusion from the Camp and related activities because they had not previously experienced being unilaterally deprived of power by women. Heterosexual women, who were still in the process of working out their position, felt undermined by the charges of lesbianism which formed part of the media's smear campaign lamenting the demise of family ties. The media's stance played upon and compounded their feelings of guilt at 'abandoning' their children and menfolk. The schisms amongst Greenham's supporters both inside and outside the Base made it easier for the media to condemn

Greenham women for doing their own thing, even if this included ultimately nurturing the whole world by preventing its destruction through nuclear war.

Collective, egalitarian relations became the Greenham women's hallmark as they struggled against state harassment and physical deprivation. Working cooperatively enabled women to assert their power both individually and collectively. Individual women were encouraged to reach their own decisions about their involvement in Greenham activities and not be coerced by group cohesion and dynamics into adopting decisions others made on their behalf. Participative democracy created the ethos in which they worked, lived and played. They were assertive and confident without being aggressive. Nonviolence was their counter to violence (Feminism and Non-Violence Study Group, 1983).

The Greenham women were unclear about their long-term strategy but, they knew they had to redefine both politics, by grasping the initiative from the state which had set the parameters around the nuclear debate, and the problem, by focusing the issue sharply and simply on Cruise's lethal potential. This they hoped would reach the heart and minds of people typically uninvolved in politics and rouse them through a process of self-discovery to a consciousness of the threat hanging over them and their power to challenge the state's decision.

The Greenham women furthered their objective of supplanting the state's position by contrasting the destructive anti-life potential of nuclear weapons with the celebration of everyday life. Their persistent refusal to vacate their Camp, making it their home against all odds, and calling for mass action bringing together for public display, fragments of ordinary existence pregnant with meaning and validating everyday reality for the individuals concerned, became the embodiment of this principle in practice. Photos of loved ones and other memorabilia formed symbols of protest adorning the perimeter fence at Greenham. The symbolic juxtaposition of daily joy and life with the slaughter of war achieved prominence during mass actions. The encircling of the Base by 30,000 women and their individual statements in December 1982 was an extremely powerful demonstration of the fusion between society's political existence and the impact of its decision-making processes on people's personal everyday lives.

Having women individually develop their own spaces and statements increased their sense of participation and confidence in this mass project. Acting in accordance with the principles of women personally determining their contribution to the struggle also ensured that the definition of the situation was one they had created rather than one determined by others and imposed on them. Each woman's statement was a personalised comment embedded in her beliefs. Conducting their action on these premises also facilitated women sharing their personal consciousness and fears with others. It was also a way of maximising the impact of the limited resources available to the group. The action at Greenham revealed that a nonviolent, collective show of strength and quiet determination was possible and could be influential. It also popularised Greenham women's vision of a peaceful world. This contrasted sharply with the aggressive man-made one the state was peddling (Cook and Kirk, 1983).

Small group discussions and workshops were the main forums Greenham women used to consider their action, take decisions about its exact nature and identify their individual contribution to it. Following principles of feminist nonviolence, women discussed and examined the law, the possibility of their arrest and the precautions they could take to ensure their physical and emotional safety (Cook and Kirk, 1983).

Networking was an important means through which Greenham women acquired influence which went beyond the numbers living at the camp and surpassed national boundaries. This enabled them to receive financial and moral support from women in other countries and encourage the creation of other women-only peace camps. Networking is an important means through which community work can transcend its own parochial boundaries and augment its resources in non-competitive ways.

The powerful nature of their working methodology has been evident in all Greenham women's activities. The 'die-in' at the Stock Exchange on 7 June, 1982 provides one illustration of its expression in practice. In the 'die-in', Greenham Women demonstrated how easily women can release their creativity and make political statements through the artifacts of everyday life. Small self-selected decentralised groups planned the 'die-in' and facilitated the processes through which individuals proceeded to develop their personal contribution to the collective undertaking. The working principles enshrined in the relationships fostered within these groups promoted a form of organisation which empowered rather than deskilled women. Individual women were supported when they voiced their fears about being run over, verbally abused or in conflict with the law. No woman was coerced by others into taking on more than she felt personally able to handle. Nor was she made to feel guilty for drawing boundaries around the extent of her involvement and sticking to feeling comfortable with her contribution. As indicated above, these principles also underpinned Greenham women's mass actions.

Greenham women's challenge to the state's definitions of the Cruise problem quickly generated enormous support for and mobilised large numbers of people in favour of unilateral nuclear disarmament. Its position was adopted formally by the Labour Party and put before the electorate during the 1985 general election. Though Labour failed to achieve electoral victory, its programme was endorsed by about one-third of those voting, showing a significant proportion of the British populace endorsed this stance. Greenham women's influence spread to the broader peace movement in Britain, especially CND and END and inspired organisations concerned with other issues, for example, the 'March for Jobs Campaign' and captured the imagination of sundry individuals.

Those moved by the Greenham women's actions implemented many of their ideas and practices in their own organisations. The mixed peace movement became more aware of gender oppression and adopted many of the methods used by the Greenham women in its own work (Dominelli, 1986b). For example, the impact of Greenham was particularly evident in demonstrations it sponsored during the Easter period in 1983. Nonviolent direct action and the linking of personal experiences with political decisions made by a small caucus of politicians featured prominently in these.

Moreover, organisations like CND promoted the work of Greenham women by asking them to speak to their members and share the lessons gained from their way of organising. Besides helping the membership in other groups, such contact enabled Greenham women to engage in further consciousness-raising, sharing their views with others and obtaining both moral and material support for their cause. Many women from these other organisations joined in the major protests taking place at Greenham.

The growing public support for Greenham women and the penetration of their ideas and methods to other organisations made the state fear the powers which could be unleashed by the Greenham women. The state launched a concerted counter-offensive which encouraged women to form hierarchically structured 'peace groups' endorsing the NATO decision, for example, Families for Peace. These groupings were unable to attract either mass public sympathy or large numbers of women.

The state also initiated a massive media campaign disparaging Greenham women and belittling their concerns. It placed a powerful government minister in charge of its media onslaught and propaganda against them. The state also intensified the harassment of Greenham women, although they had already undergone frequent evictions from their camp and the destruction of their 'benders' (tents constructed of plastic sheets). State harassment was intensified as legal processes swung into action against them. In some instances, local bye-laws were changed to deal with their presence. Legal intimidation of Greenham women also included their being denied voting rights and access to social security benefits.

The physical security of the Base was also strengthened in recognition of the damage which could be caused by a few committed women acting without offensive weapons. Barbed wire was placed around the perimeter fence and policing assumed a higher profile. Vast sums of public money were invested in these

117

measures as the state tried to redefine the issue of Greenham as a matter of 'law and order'. Evidence has also emerged to suggest that 'ray guns' have been used to repel the women camping at its gates (Beasley, 1986). 'Star Wars' had become a reality for the women at Greenham.

The state's response ultimately signalled the weaknesses of the Greenham women's approach, despite its replication in peace camps in Italy, Iceland, Australia and America. Relying almost exclusively on resources generated amongst themselves and their supporters, Greenham women could not shift the balance of power existing between themselves and the state. Yet, they needed to do this if they were to succeed in reversing state policy. Like other feminist initiatives in the political arena, Greenham demonstrates the importance of having a feminist presence in both local and central state structures, the trade union movement and society more generally for its achievements to be sustained over lengthy periods of time. Another weakness of the Greenham women's approach stemmed from their analysis of patriarchy. Identifying *men's* construction of the social order as the problem held the danger of seeing 'men' as the enemy rather than patriarchal social relations, and could by ignoring men's contribution to the struggle for peace allow men to continue reinforcing oppressive relations. Some feminists, for example, black feminists Angela Davis (1989) and Bell Hooks (1984) argue that men, particularly working class men, have a crucial role to play in the peace movement because the war movement is advanced by capitalist social relations which oppress working class men and women. The question of the nature of the relationship between men and feminist social action is problematic and has yet to be addressed adequately. Additionally, the polarisation of values into negative values held by men and positive ones embraced by women runs the risk of endorsing biological determinism. It also ignores the merging of people's value systems in reality, and the roles women play in reinforcing patriarchal relations when conforming to dominant ideological norms. In other words, both men and women support capitalist patriarchal relations and it is these which both men and women have to eradicate in creating egalitarian relationships between them.

The Impact of the Greenham Women's Peace Movement on Traditional Community Action

Widespread public exposure in the media, the involvement of thousands of women community activists in Greenham Common activities, and the talks Greenham women have had with community groups have meant that the ideas and forms of organisation initiated by a nucleus of women as Greenham Common have filtered through to a large number of people active in more traditional types of community work. Greenham women's contribution has highlighted the development of a new strand of community action which has questioned traditional forms of community organisation. Particularly relevant in this context are the accepted relationships between the organisers and the organised, community workers' expectations about group dynamics and traditional concepts of locality based organising. By compelling community workers to re-examine their traditional positions, Greenham women have provided a catalyst for changing the nature of community work. Revitalising methods of organising has been especially noticeable in community work amongst women who have supported Greenham events, for example, the Coventry Women's Health Network (CWHN, 1985).

Community workers can pick up on the experience of empowerment which flows from feminist work in small groups like those fostered at Greenham. Most people feel uninvolved in key decisions affecting community life, for example, school closures, factory relocations, the destruction of the local environment, and absence of leisure facilities. People can redefine their aspirations for their communities by wresting the initiative from the state and powerful others seeking to problematise their existence. Redefining their lives requires people to raise their individual consciousness and make explicit connections between macrolevel political processes and the microcosm within which they lead personal lives.

Community work allegedly embarks on such processes. However, it usually does this within the parameters of traditional thought which do not challenge established modes of action. Foremost amongst these are the separation of an issue from its total social context; and the rule of economic criteria rather than social ones in political decision-making processes. Additionally, bureaucratic procedures are used to manipulate discussions and hinder free flowing creativity (see Alinsky, 1970). The conduct of a public meeting considering the demolition of housing for road construction is illustrative of the restrictive methodology prevailing in traditional community work. People attending it are left feeling frustrated and angry because they have been treated as passive participants and their concerns have failed to achieve prominence in the proceedings. There has been no fusion between the political and the personal and no connection made between remote political decision-making and people's daily lives. Aggressive posturing rather than a true confrontation of the issues at stake has been reinforced (Dominelli, 1986b).

Other facets of the Greenham women's approach to community action encompass the following:

* The creation of women-only spaces to empower women;
* Challenging gender stereotypes by ensuring that men do not grab all the powerful decision-making positions such as being

119

chairperson, highlighting womens' capacity to take and role in making decisions; having men undertake nurturing tasks such as making the tea and minding the children; and freeing women's energies to assume other responsibilities; and

* Altering worker-group interaction by endorsing collective group dynamics which eliminate hierarchical relationships between community workers and the group they are working with and provide individuals with the space to reach their own decisions.

Working along Greenham woman's lines makes community workers more accountable to community groups. Community workers continue playing a role in initiating ideas, but do so as group members and participate in implementing action on the same basis as everyone else. Community workers must endorse collective working, sharing of skills and participatory mechanisms, refuel group commitment to the task at hand and boost group morale. In developing groups consonant with feminist practice, community workers encouraaaaaage people to use their own skills and assume personal responsibility for the decisions each takes as a member of the group.

Moreover, community workers can facilitate the liberation of thought by enabling people to become involved in consciousness-raising exercises which help them redefine their personal reality in social terms. In these, people can give expression to affective responses and emotions, thereby connecting external decision-making with their personal experiences.

Community workers can further the elimination of the sexist domestic division of labour. Confronting the constraints familial ideology places on women enables community workers to play an active role in overcoming barriers to women's participation in protests. They can also encourage men to assume nurturing roles and childcare duties. Facilitating such activities enables community work to tackle social divisions which inhibit collective community responses and move people into forming non-oppressive relationships. Additionally they would be resisting the subordination of welfare needs to economic exigencies. Working in non-oppressive ways necessitates posing the following critical questions:

* What are the implications of particular actions for black and other oppressed peoples?
* How do these implications differ from those of the group I'm working with?
* Why?
* How do we allow for these in our activities?

Community workers will encounter state hostility if they begin organising to challenge either state power or the hegemony of the dominant ideology. Preparing for a negative state response requires community workers to build extensive networks with overwhelming public support locally, nationally and internationally. Both public and personal resources must be mobilised in favour of its cause. Community work is well placed to develop along these lines because it has a community base through which links can emanate from the locality outward.

Community work can confront the state through nonviolent action, but it must develop extensive support bases and form alliances beforehand. It can endorse collective ways of working, although these may be problematic. Finally, consciousness raising is a powerful medium, but its impact on community work will be limited if groups do not acquire the resources and widespread support they need to translate awareness into action promoting fundamental social change. Only by securing these can community work avoid losing the circumscribed gains currently characterising feminist community action as exemplified by the Greenham Women's Peace Movement (Dominelli, 1986b).

Chapter 6
Conclusions

Organising Women in the Community

Patriarchal relations prevailing in society have also been reflected in community work. Though women have played key roles in undertaking community action defending humanitarian, caring values in the community and maintaining working class standards of living, the value of their contribution has been consistently underrated. Only occasionally does the community work literature recognise this reality, for example, Mayo's (1977) *Women in the Community* and give due emphasis to women's involvement in general community issues. It is almost as if women were invisible, operating only in supporting roles behind the scenes. Yet, women have historically played significant roles in community action, for example, in the crucial housing struggles which were waged over rent controls in Glasgow in 1915 (Mayo, 1972; Ginsburg, 1979).

More recently, a growing women's liberation movement and women's increasing consciousness over their position, has led women to organise with other women over issues of major concern to their welfare, for example, the physical assault of women within intimate relationships, the sexual assault of women, women's emotional well-being. Supporting women through these traumas has preoccupied the National Women's Aid Federation, Women's Rape Crisis Centres, and feminist therapists, respectively. By undertaking gender-specific action, women have been able to expose the material hardship and emotional suffering which permeates their lives. They have also revealed the constraints imposed on women's ability to organise and care for themselves by the overwhelming burden of family responsibilities they carry, and their financial dependency on male partners. These constraints receive their legitimacy in the marriage contract, state legislation, particularly that concerning social security, taxation, and pensions, and the opportunities and facilities made available to waged and unwaged women.

Community activists intending to organise with women need to understand these structural constraints and facilitate women's handling of them in their practice and take practical steps which nurture their willingness to meet with others and organise over common issues. Community workers should be prepared to dissolve the distinction between professionals and ordinary group members by undertaking role reversals which have them as professionals servicing lay people. For example, community workers preparing the tea whilst the women meet, men minding the children. Community workers should also aim to make themselves redundant by ensuring that the group with which they are working quickly assumes responsibility for its decision-making and acquires the skills necessary for conducting its business.

However, when organising with women in the community, it is not enough just to organise women in small groups, though these are essential if women are to understand their personal experiences, sharpen their demands, develop their confidence, and raise their consciousness about the social position of women. At some point, the connection between the social organisation of their reality and their personal experiences must be made in political terms. Only then can gender oppression be substantially challenged. For this to become widespread, women will have to form alliances with others outside their group. These outsiders may be trade unionists, politicans, professionals, men and women involved in voluntary organisations. As the British experience of feminists working in the local state fostering anti-racist and anti-sexist initiatives and American feminists' lengthy struggle over reproductive rights have revealed, it is vital that limited feminist gains are underpinned by this broader support if they are to withstand determined anti-feminist opposition (Adamson *et al*, 1988). Moreover, such support has to encompass the central state which must also be permeated by a feminist political presence if it is to underwrite social change at all the other levels of society. When seeking alliances with others to maximise the group's strength and increase its numerical standing, it is important to ensure that the feminist group is not incorporated by those with whom it seeks alliances. Otherwise, it will lose its own political thrust and independent impact.

Organising with women in the community is not an easy task, given that women are isolated from one another in the workplace and when performing their domestic tasks at home. However, feminists have demonstrated that these obstacles are not impossible to overcome. Women's involvement in homeworkers campaigns (Hopkins, 1982), housing campaigns (Mayo, 1977), campaigns around issues concerning single-parent families (Mayo, 1977), older women's campaigns (Doress and Siegal, 1987), health campaigns (Ruzek, 1978; Doyal, 1983), nuclear disarmament (Cook and Kirk, 1983), and workplace issues (Benn and Sedgely, 1984), provide testimonials to women's organising abilities and supportive actions. Women will come together to fight for their interests, if the forms of organising used are those which pick up on their needs as *women organising*. Women's resilience in struggle

123

has been evident in women workers' industrial action. Some of the most protracted struggles on the wage labour front in recent times have been mounted and sustained by women, for example, Mansfield Hosiery, Imperial Typewriters, Grunwick, Chix, Lee Jeans, Kigass. Nevertheless, community workers organising with women walk a tightrope. They must ensure that their activities do not ghettoise organising with women and relegate it to second place. Preventing this from occurring is crucial if organising with women is not to be subsumed by male prerogative and operate as an extension of the male community worker's preserve. Additionally, the welfare needs of women community workers has to be addressed. Safeguarding their interests entails considering their waged work and domestic commitments, ensuring equality of opportunity and recognising their specific contributions to organising. Many of the rights women demand in both their working and domestic life, for example, the right to an independent income, a violence-free existence and personal well-being, are as relevant to children and men as they are to women.

Feminist community action has advanced the welfare of children, women and men. But its achievements have also suffered reverses, and its goal of eliminating gender oppression remains as distant as ever. However, the progress which has taken place has maintained women's morale and encouraged their continued struggle for their rights, a humanity-oriented world and social justice. It has also affirmed women's conviction that there is nothing 'natural' about their subordinate position, and that the fatalistic outlook which follows from this is inimical to their interests. Women can and do act to promote their vision of the world. But they must work at making it a reality. Gender equality will not magically feature on the world's agenda when a classless society is reached if the issue is not directly addressed.

Feminist Community Action and the Future

Feminist community action appears to have increased relevancy to people caught in a web of declining welfare services, rising joblessness, and diminished civil and human rights as cost-conscious governments seek to repress people's resistance to oppressive social relations through both 'hard' and 'soft' forms of social control and claw back earlier feminist gains, for example, women's reproductive rights in America; women's employment protection and social benefits in Britain. Women are organising in the community, albeit on a self-help basis to promote their interests. The following principles which feminists use in guiding their activities are relevant to all community workers irrespective of the gender of group members because they aim to eliminate hierarchy and relations of dominance throughout society.

Feminist Theory and Practice: Guiding Principles

* Developing an individual's full potential;
* Eliminating gender oppression;
* Transforming social relations in egalitarian directions;
* Fostering the well-being of all women in society regardless of their social status, including class, 'race', sexual orientation, age, or physical or mental capacities;
* Acknowledging the political nature of all social relations;
* Promoting egalitarian relations between men and women, adults and children;
* Increasing women's control over their lives;
* Having a right to welfare;
* Making caring a collective responsibility which is undertaken by both men and women;
* Acknowledging the interconnectedness between the public and private spheres;
* Ensuring that work, whether carried out in the home or the workplace provides women with choices about what they are doing, how they are doing it, and why they are doing it;
* Democratising institutional decision-making processes;
* Promoting nonviolent approaches to resolving conflicts;
* Shifting public priorities and resources in favour of meeting human needs; and
* Highlighting the interconnectedness between social policy and economic policy and ensuring that social policy is not subordinated to economic exigencies.

In practical terms these principles have led feminists to demand that:

* The social causes of individual hardship and unbalanced emotional development be recognised;
* Individuals not be pathologised for their plight;
* Egalitarianism permeate all social interaction;
* Public institutions and organisations foster individual and collective well-being;
* Sexism in all its forms be eliminated from individual behaviour, social institutions, social policy, cultural values and social norms;
* All forms of oppression be eliminated;
* All individuals be publicly guaranteed an existence free from violence and coercion;
* All individuals be provided with a publicly guaranteed minimum income;
* Women have a right to an independent income;
* Masculinity and femininity be redefined in non-oppressive ways;
* Familial ideology be redefined in ways compatible with egalitarian relations between 'family' members;

* A diversity of 'family' forms be recognised;
* Parenting be recognised as a social activity and responsibility;
* Working relations be transformed to provide all workers with equality of status, pay, and humane conditions of work;
* Hierarchy in the division of labour be eliminated;
* The state facilitate people's need to develop personal, familial and community relationships;
* The provision of goods and services which foster women's creative talents and potential;
* Social planning reflect social needs and involve users of the services and workers in their formulation;
* Prevention of avoidable material and emotional distress be given priority in planning social services and health care systems; and
* Professionalism be redefined to reflect the interests of the users of the service.

Feminists have sought to incorporate these demands in their own practice at both the strategic and tactical levels. This has resulted in

* creating prefigurative forms of the social relations they envisage for the future in their current practice; and
* forming alliances with others to eliminate social injustice.

Though feminist community action falls short of achieving feminists' ultimate goal of transforming society and redistributing power and resources in egalitarian directions, feminist action is likely to have two immediate beneficial effects. One of these is that feminist activities are likely to provide women, and to some extent children and men, with some improvement in their material conditions, even if in the hostile climate currently created by the 'New Right' that is to safeguard their present position. In the face of the serious deterioration in the standards of living of women, black people and the working class, defending past gains is a worthy endeavour although care needs to be taken to ensure that this defensive stance does not become a substitute for the goal of transforming social relations. The second effect is the positive influence that struggling for progress has had on women's consciousness, and in consequence on that of children and men. Included in this are firstly,

* the exposure of current myths of equality which disguise society's unequal distribution of resources and the degradation of marginalised groups like women, black people, and large sections of the working class in the capitalist social system and, secondly,
* the feeling of power and confidence achieved by powerless groups who challenge their ascribed position in society by acting collectively.

At the level of the community, therefore, women and other marginalised groups are organising against their oppression with some degree of success in demanding both changes in existing provisions for them and the creation of services previously missing.

The state seems to be withdrawing its support of community action, particularly its more challenging versions, in favour of funding more traditional forms of community work, for example, community organisation and community care, although even these are inadequately financed for the tasks set for them. However, these restrictions have not totally succeeded in protecting the state from the impact of community action, including feminist community action. Many social workers, as state employees, are forming alliances with community groups in their endeavours to provide users with more appropriate services. Welfare workers' idealistic fervour and commitment to helping people aptly lend themselves to those wishing to facilitate the process whereby the powerless organise to take control of their own lives.

Feminist community action is riddled with contradictions at whatever level it is operating. But because it heralds the dawning of a new non-oppressive social order, feminist community action is a sphere of activity of significance to all those intent on promoting people's welfare. Traditional community workers need to take note of its potential and make its theory and practice their own.

Bibliography

Abrams, P. (1980) Social Change, Social Networks and Neighbourhood Care, in *Social Work Service*, 22, pp. 12–23.

Achilles Heel Collective (AHC) (1983) *Achilles Heel Special Issue on Masculinity*, No. 5, London: ACH.

Adams, A. L. (1989) There's No Place Like Home: On the Place of Identity Politics in *Feminist Review*, No. 31, Spring, pp. 22–34.

Adamson, N., Briskin, L. and McPhail, M. (1988) *Organising for Change: The Contemporary Women's Movement in Canada*. Oxford: Oxford University Press.

Ahmed, S., Cheetham, J., and Small, J. (1987) *Social Work with Black Children and their Families*. London: Batsford.

Alcock, P., Cochrane, A., and Lee, P. (1984) Interviewing John Bennington, in *Critical Social Policy*, Issue 9, Spring, pp. 69–87.

Alcock, P. (1989) Why Citizenship and Welfare Rights Offer New Hope for Welfare in Britain, in *Critical Social Policy*, Issue 26, Autumn, pp. 32–43.

Aldred, C. (1981) *Women at Work*, London: Pan.

Alinsky, S. (1969) *Reveille for Radicals*. New York: Vintage Books.

Alinsky, S. (1971) *Rules for Radicals*, New York: Random House.

Allen, S., Sanders, L., and Wallis, J. (eds.) (1974) *Conditions of Illusion*. Leeds: Feminist Books.

Amos, A., and Parmar, P. (1984) Challenging Imperial Feminism, in *Feminist Review*, No. 17, pp. 3–17.

Andors, P. (1983) *The Unfinished Liberation of Chinese Women: 1949–1980*. Brighton: Wheatsheaf Books.

Armstrong, J. (1977) *Analysis of the Inner Area Partnership Scheme Applications*, Paper for the Leicester Community Work Unit Management Meeting. Leicester: CWTU.

Armstrong, J., and Gill, K. (1978) The Unitary Approach: What Relevance for Community Work? in *Social Work Today*, Vol, 10, No. 11, 7 November.

Armstrong, L. (1987) *Kiss Daddy Goodnight*. New York: Random House.

Armstrong, P. (1984) *Labour Pains: Women's Work in Crisis*. Toronto: Women's Press.

Ashurst, P. and Hall, Z. (1989) *Women in Distress*. London: Tavistock Routledge.

Asian Sheltered Residential Accommodation (ASRA) (1981) *Asians Sheltered Residential Accommodation*. London: ASRA.

Atkin, K., Cameron, E., Badger, F., Evers, H. (1989) Asian Elders: Knowledge and Future Use of Community Social and Health Services in *New Community*, Vol, 15, No. 3, April 1989.

Audit Commission (1986) *Making a Reality of Community Care*. Norwich: HMSO.

Baker Miller, J. (1976) *Toward a New Psychology of Women*. Boston: Beacon Press.

Baldwin, S. (1985) *The Cost of Caring*. London: Routledge and Kegan Paul.

Bailey, R., and Brake, R. (1975) *Radical Social Work*. London: Routledge and Kegan Paul.

Baine, S. (1975) *Community Action and Local Government*. London: G. Bell and Sons.

Baldock, P. (1974) *Community Work and Social work*. London: Routledge and Kegan Paul.

Baldock, P. (1977) Why Community Action? The Historical Origins of the Radical Trend in British Community Work in *The Community Development Journal*, 2(1) April, pp. 68–79.

Baldock, P. (1979) A Historical Review of Community Work, 1968–1978 in *The Community Development Journal*, pp. 172–181.

Barclay, P. M. (1982) *(The Barclay Report) Social Workers: Their Role and Tasks*. London: Bedford Square Press.

Barker, D. L. and Allen, S. (eds.) (1976) *Sexual Divisions and Society: Process and Change*. London: Tavistock.

Barker, H. (1986) Recapturing Sisterhood: A Critical Look at 'Process' in Feminist Organising and Community Work in *Critical Social Policy*. Issue 16, Summer, pp. 80–90.

Barratt Brown, M. (1984) *Models in Political Economy*. London: Penguin Books.

Barrett, M. (1981) *Women's Oppression Today. Problems on Marxist Feminism Analysis*. London: Verso.

Barrett, M. and McIntosh, M. (1982) *The Anti-Social Family*. London: Verso.

Barrett, M. and McIntosh, M. (1985) Ethnocentrism and Socialist-Feminist Theory in *Feminist Review*, No. 20, pp.

Batten, T. with Batten, M. (1957) *Communities and their Development*. Oxford: Oxford University Press.

Batten, T. (1986) *The Human Factor in Community Work*. Oxford: Oxford University Press.

Batten, T. (1967) *The Non-Directive Approach in Group and Community Work*. Oxford: Oxford University Press.

Beasley, K. (1986) Who's Zapping Who? in *Spare Rib*, No. 166, May, pp. 10–11.

Belden, J. (1970) *China Shakes the World*. New York: Monthly Review Press.

Bell, C., and Newby, H. (1971) *Community Studies*, London: Allen

& Unwin.

Bell, S. (1988) *When Salem Came to the Boro*. London: Pan Books.

Benhabib, S. and Cornell, D. (eds.) (1987) *Feminism as Critique*. Minneapolis: University of Minnesota Press.

Benn, M. and Sedley, A. (1982) *Sexual Harassment at Work*. London: National Council for Civil Liberties.

Bennington, J. (1976) *Local Government Becomes Big Business*. London: Community Development Projects.

Benwell Community Project (1978) *The Making of a Ruling Class: Benwell Community Project Final Report Series 6*. Newcastle: Benwell Community Project.

Benyon, M. (1989) *Report on Gender and the Education System Study Day*. Warwick University Senate Sex Equality Committee, May.

Bettleheim, B. (1970) *The Children of the Dream*. New York: Avon.

Beuret, K., and Stoker, G. (1986) The Labour Party and Neighbourhood Decentralisation: Flirtation or Commitment? in *Critical Social Policy*, Issue 17, Autumn, pp. 4–21.

Bhavnani, K. and Coulson, M. (1986) Transforming Socialist-Feminism: The Challenge of Racism in *Feminist Review*, No. 23, Summer, pp. 81–92.

Bhat, A., Carr-Hill, R., Ohri, S. (eds.) (1988) *Britain's Black Population*. London: Gower.

Biddle, L. and Biddle, W. (1965) *The Community Development Process: The Rediscovery of Local Initiative*. New York: Holt, Rinehart and Winston.

Billingsley, A., and Giovannoni, (1972) *Children of the Storm: Black Children and Child Welfare*. New York: Harcourt Brace Jovanovich.

Binney, V, Harkell, G., and Nixon, J. (1981) *Leaving Violent Men: A Study of Refuges and Housing for Battered Women*. London: Women's Aid Federation.

Blagg, H., and Derricourt, N. (1982) Why We Need to Reconstruct a Theory of the State for Community Work in *Community Work and the State* edited by Craig *et al.* London: Routledge & Kegan Paul.

Bolger, S., Corrigan, P. Docking, J., and Frost, N. (1981) *Towards Socialist Welfare Work*. London: Macmillan.

Bonny, S. (1984) *Who Cares in Southwark*. London: National Association of Carers and Their Elderly Dependents.

Bornat, J., Phillipson, C., and Ward, S. (1985) *A Manifesto for Old Age*. London: Pluto Press.

Boston Women's Health Collective (BWHC) (1979) *Our Bodies, Ourselves*. New York: Simon and Schuster.

Bowl, R. (1985) *Changing the Nature of Masculinity – A Task for Social Work*. Monograph, Norwich: The University of East Anglia.

Bradley, M. *et al* (1971) *Unbecoming Men: A Men's Consciousness Raising Group Writes on Oppression and Themselves*. New York: Times Change Press.

Braeger, G. and Purcell, F. (1967) *Community Action Against Poverty*. New Haven: New Haven College and University Press.

Braeger, G. and Specht, H. (1969) Mobilising the Poor for Social Action in *Readings in Community Organisation Practice* edited by Kramer and Specht. Englewood Cliffs: Prentice-Hall.

Brah, A. (1988/89) Black Struggles, Equality and Education, in *Critical Social Policy*, Issue, 24, Winter, pp. 83–89.

Brailey, M. (1986) Splitting up – and Finding Somewhere to Live, in *Critical Social Policy*, Issue, 17, Autumn, pp. 60–69.

Brandwein, R. (1987) Women and Community Organisation in *The Woman Client: Providing Human Services in a Changing World* edited by Burden and Gottlieb. London: Tavistock.

Braverman, H. (1974–) *Labor and Monopoly Capital. The Degradation of Work in the Twentieth Century*. New York: Monthly Review Press.

Bridges, L. (1975) The Ministry of Internal Security: British Urban Social Policy: 1968–1974 in *Race and Class*, Vol. 16, No. 4, pp. 376–389.

Brook, E. and Davis, A. (1985) *Women, the Family and Social Work*. London: Tavistock.

Brown, G. and Harris, T. (1978) *The Social Origins of Depression*. London: Tavistock.

Brownmiller, S. (1976) *Against our Will*. London: Penguin.

Bruegel, I. (1989) Sex and Race in the Labour Market in *Feminist Review*, No. 32, Summer, pp. 49–68.

Bryan, B., Dadzie, S., Scafe, S. (1985) *The Heart of the Race*. London: Virago.

Burden, D. S. and Gottlieb, N. (1987) *The Woman Client: Providing Human Services in a Changing World*. London: Tavistock.

Buynan, T. (1977) *The History and Practice of the Political Police in Britain*. London: Quartet Books.

Cameron, E. and Badger, F. (1985) Old, Needy and Black in *Nursing Times*, Vol. 84, No. 32, 10 August.

Campbell, B. (1980) Feminist Sexual Politics in *Feminist Review*, No. 5, pp. 1–18.

Campbell, B. *et al* (1986) Feminism and Class Politics, in *Feminist Review*, No. 23, pp. 13–30.

Campling, J. (1981) *Images of Ourselves: Women with Disabilities Talking*. London: Routledge & Kegan Paul.

Carby, H. (1982) White Woman Listen! Black Feminism and the Boundaries of Sisterhood in *The Empire Strikes Back* edited by Centre for Contemporary and Cultural Studies. London: Hutchinson.

Carpenter, V., Hart, L., and Salvat, G. (1982) Working with Girls, in *Women in Collective Action*, edited by Curno *et al*. London: Association of Community Workers, pp. 140–147.

Castles, S. and Kosak, G. (1972) The Function of Labour Immigration in Western European Capitalism in *New Left Re-*

131

view, 73, May/June, pp. 8–21.

Cavendish, R. (1982) *Women on the Line*. London: Routledge and Kegan Paul.

Centre for Contemporary and Cultural Studies (CCCS) (1982) *The Empire Strikes Back*. London: Hutchinson.

Chapman, R. and Rutherford, J. (1988) *Male Order: Unwrapping Masculinity*. London: Lawrence and Wishart.

Cheetham, J. (1982) *Ethnicity and Social Work*. Oxford: Oxford University Press.

Coard, B. 91971) *How West Indian Children Are Made Educationally Subnormal*. London: New Beacon Books.

Cochrane, M., Miller, J., Tetlow, K., and Stiles, J. (1982) South London Community Health Projects in *Women in Collective Action* edited by Curno *et al*, London: Association of Community Workers, pp. 113–129.

Cockburn, C. (1977a) *The Local State*. London: Pluto Press.

Cockburn, C. (1977b) When Women Get Involved in Community Action, in *Women in the Community*, edited by Mayo. London: Routledge & Kegan Paul, pp. 61–70.

Cockburn, C. (1981) The Material of Male Power, *Feminist Review*, No. 9.

Cockburn, C. (1983) *Brothers: Male Dominance and Technological Change*. London: Pluto Press.

Cockburn, C. (1986) *Machinery of Dominance: Women, Men and Technical Know-How*. London: Pluto Press.

Cohen, L. (1984) *Small Expectation – Society's Betrayal of Older Women*. Toronto: McLelland and Stewart.

Comer, J. P. and Poussaint, A. P. (1975) *Black Child Care*, New York: Pocket Books.

Comer, L. (1974) *Wedlocked Women*. Leeds: Feminist Press.

Community Action: *Investigator's Handbook*.

Community Action: Issue No. 45.

Community Development Project Working Group (CDPWG) (1974) The British National Community Development Project, 1969–1974 in *The Community Development Journal*, 9(6), October, pp. 162–184.

Community Development Projects (CDP) (1975) *The Poverty of the Improvement Programme*. London: CDP.

Community Development Projects (CDP) (1975) *Workers on the Scrapheap*.

Community Development Projects (CDP) (1976) *The Limits of the Law*. London: CDP.

Community Development Projects (CDP) (1976) *Profits Against Houses*. London: CDP.

Community Development Projects (CDP) (1976) *Whatever Happened to Council Housing?* London: CDP.

Community Development Projects (CDP) (1977a) *The Costs of Industrial Change*. London: CDP.

Community Development Projects (CDP) (1977b) *Gilding the Ghetto*. London: CDP.

Community Development Projects (CDP) (1977c) *The Limits of the Law*. London: CDP.

Conference of Socialist Economists (CSE) (1976) *Housing and Class in Britain*. London: CSE.

Connell, R. W. (1983) *Which Way is Up? Essays on Class, Sex and Culture*. Sydney: Allen and Unwin.

Conrad, P., and Kern, R. (eds.) (1981) *The Sociology of Health and Illness: Critical Perspectives*. New York: St. Martin's Press.

Connelly, P. (1979) *Last Hired, First Fired: Women and the Canadian Workforce*. Toronto: The Women's Press.

Cook, A., and Kirk, G. (1983) *Greenham Women Everywhere*. London: Pluto Press.

Cooper, M. (1980) Normanton: Interweaving Social Work and the Community in *Going Local* edited by Hadley and McGrath. London: Bedford Square Press.

Coote, A., and Campbell, B. (1982) *Sweet Freedom*. London: Pan Books.

Counter Information Service. (1978) *Paying for the Crisis*. Report No. 18.

Coventry Women's Health Network (CWHN) (1985) Discussions with members of the CWHN During 1984–85.

Cowley, J. (1977) *Community or Class*. London: Stage One/ Routledge & Kegan Paul.

Cox, F., Erlich, J., Rothman, J., and Tropman, J. (eds) (1970) *Strategies of Community Organisation*. Itaska, Il.: Peacock Publishing.

Coyle, A. (1984) *Redundant Women*. London: The Women's Press.

Coyle, A., and Skinner, J. (1988) *Women and Work: Positive Action for Change*. London: Macmillan, 1988.

Crean, S. (1988) *In the Name of the Fathers: The Story Behind Child Custody*. Toronto: Amanita Publications.

Craig, G. (1989) Community Work and the State in *The Community Development Journal*, 26(4), pp. 3–18.

Craig, G., Derricourt, N., and Loney, M. (1982) *Community Work and the State: Towards a Radical Practice*. London: Routledge & Kegan Paul.

Croft, S., and Beresford, P. (1986) *Whose Welfare? Private Care or Public Services*. Brighton: Lewis Cohen Urban Studies Centre, Brighton Polytechnic.

Croft, S., and Beresford, P. (1989) User-involvement, Citizenship and Social Policy, in *Critical Social Policy*, Issue, 26, Autumn, pp. 5–18.

Curno, A., Lamming, A., Leach, L., Stiles, J., Ward, V., Wright, A., and Ziff, T. (1982) *Women in Collective Action*. London: Association of Community Workers.

Curno, P. (1978) *Political Issues in Community Work*. London: Routledge & Kegan Paul.

Dale, J. and Derricourt, N. (1990) Dilemmas in Housing Oriented Community Work? in *The Community Development Journal* 25 (2), pp. 66–74.

Dale, J. and Foster, P. (1986) *Feminists and State Welfare*. London: Routledge & Kegan Paul.

Dalla Costa, M. and James, S. (1972) *The Power of Women and the Subversion of the Community*. Bristol: Falling Wall Press.

Daniel, S. (1988) A Code for Elders in *Social Work Today*, 18 August.

D'Ardenne, P. and Mahtani, A. (1989) *Transcultural Counselling in Action*. London: Sage.

Daullah, M. (1989) Racism, Probation and Promotion Prospects in *NAPO News*, No. 7. February.

David, M. and New, C. (1985) *For the Children's Sake: Making Childcare more than Women's Business*. London: Penguin.

Davis, R. (1988) Learning from Working Class Women in *The Community Development Journal*, 23(2), pp. 110–116.

Davies, W. (1982) A Women's Group – A Case Study to Think About, in *Women's Collective Action*, edited by Curno, *et al*, London: Association of Community Workers, pp. 89–102.

Davis, A. (1989) *Women, Culture and Politics*. New York: Random House.

Davis, R. (1988) Learning from Working Class Women in *The Community Development Journal*, Vol. 23, No. 2, pp. 110–116.

Davis, S. and the Committee for Abortion Rights and Against Sterilisation Abuse (1988) *Women Under Attack: Victories, Backlash and the Fight for Reproductive Freedom*. Boston: South End Press.

Deacon, B. (1983). *Social Policy and Socialism: The Struggle for Socialist Relations of Welfare*. London: Pluto Press.

Dearlove, J. (1974) The Control of Change and the Regulation of Community Action in *Community Work One* edited by Jones and Mayo. London: Routledge and Kegan Paul.

Dex, S., and Phillipson, C. (1986) Older Women in the Labour Market: A Review of Current Trends, in *Critical Social Policy*, Issue 15, Spring, pp. 79–84.

Djao, A. W. (1983) *Inequality and Social Policy, the Sociology of Social Welfare*. Toronto: John Wiley & Sons.

Dixon, G., Johnson, C., Leigh, S., and Turnbull, N. (1982) Feminist Perspectives and Practice in *Community Work and the State* edited by Craig *et al*. London: Routledge & Kegan Paul.

Dixon, J. (1990) Will Politically Inspired Community Work be Evident in 1990s? in *The Community Development Journal*, 25(2), pp. 91–101.

Dobash, R. and Dobash, R. (1979). *Violence Against Wives: A Case Against the Patriarchy*. New York: Free Press.

Docklands Development Forum (1983) *The Peoples Plan for the Docks*. London: Newham Docklands Forum.

Dominelli, L. (1974) *Autogestion* in Boufarik in *Sociologia Ruralis*. Vol. XIV, No. 4, pp. 243–260.

Dominelli, L. (1981) Violence: A Family Affair, in *Community Care*, 12 March, pp. 14–17.

Dominelli, L. (1982) *Community Action: Organising Marginalised Groups*. Reykjavik: Kwenna Frambothid.

Dominelli, L. (1986a) Father-Daughter Incest: Patriarchy's Shameful Secret in *Critical Social Policy*, No. 16, pp. 8–22.

Dominelli, L. (1986b) *Women Organising: An Analysis of Greenham Women*. Paper presented at the International Association of Schools of Social Work Congress in Tokyo, August.

Dominelli, L. (1986c) *Love and Wages*. Norwich: Novata Press.

Dominelli, L. (1986d) The Power of the Powerless: Prostitution and the Reinforcement of Submissive Femininity in *Sociological Review*, Spring, pp. 65–92.

Dominelli, L. (1988) *Anti-Racist Social Work*. London: Macmillan.

Dominelli, L. (1989) Betrayal of Trust: A Feminist Analysis of Power Relationships in Incest Abuse in *The British Journal of Social Work*, 19(4), Summer, pp. 291–307.

Dominelli, L., and Jonsdottir, G. (1988) Feminist Political Organisation: Some Reflections on the Experience of Kwenna Frambothid in Iceland, in *Feminist Review*, No. 30, Autumn, pp. 36–60.

Dominelli, L., and Leonard, P. (1982) *Power, Participation and Collective Intervention*. Report to Coventry Social Services, March.

Dominelli, L., and McLeod, E. (1989) *Feminist Social Work*. London: Macmillan.

Doress, B., and Siegal, D. L. (1987) *Ourselves, Growing Older*. New York: Simon and Schuster.

Doyal, L. (1979) *The Political Economy of Health*. London: Pluto Press.

Doyal, L. (1983) Women's Health and the Sexual Division of Labour: A Case Study of the Women's Movement in Britain in *Critical Social Policy*, Issue 7, Summer, pp. 21–33.

Doyal, L. (1985) Women and the National Health Services: The Carers and the Careless in *Women Health and Healing* edited by Lewin and Olesen. London: Tavistock Publications.

Doyal, L., and Gough, I. (1984) A Theory of Human Needs in *Critical Social Policy*, Issue 10, pp. 6–38.

Dreifus, C. (1973) *Women's Fate: Raps from a Feminist Consciousness Raising Group*. New York: Bantam Books.

Easlea, B. (1983) *Fathering the Unthinkable: Masculinity, Science and the Nuclear Arms Race*. London: Pluto Press.

Edwards, J. (1988/9) Local Government Women's Committees, in *Critical Social Policy*, Issue 24, Winter, pp. 50–64.

Edwards, J., and Batley, R. (1978) *The Politics of Positive Discrimination: An Evaluation of the Urban Programme 1967–77*. London: Tavistock.

Ehrensaft, D. (1981) When Women and Men Mother, in *Politics and Power*, No. 3. London: Routledge and Kegan Paul.

Eichenbaum, L., and Orbach, S. (1982) *Outside In, Inside Out.* London: Penguin.

Eichler, M. (1983) *Families in Canada.* Toronto: Gage.

Eichler, M. (1988) *Nonsexist Research Methods: A Practical Guide.* London: Allen & Unwin.

Eisenstein, H. (1984) *Contemporary Feminist Thought.* London: Allen and Unwin.

Eisenstein, Z. (1979) *Capitalist Patriarchy and the Case for Socialist Feminist.* New York: Monthly Review Press.

Elliott, J. L. (1979) Canadian Immigration: A Historical Assessment in Elliott, J. L. (ed.) *Two Nations, Many Cultures: Ethnic Groups in Canada.* Scarborough, Ont.: Prentice Hall.

Equal Opportunities Commission (EOC) (1984) *Carers and Services: A Comparison of Men and Women Caring for Dependent Elderly People.* Manchester: EOC.

Ernst, S., and Maguire, M. (eds.) (1987) *Living with the Sphinx – Papers from the Women's Therapy Centre.* London: The Women's Press.

Farrah, M. (1986) *Black Elders in Leicester.* Leicester: Leicester Social Services Department Report.

Feminism and Non-Violence Study Group (FNVSG) (1983) *Piecing it Together: Feminism and Non-Violence.* Buckleigh: FNVSG.

Feminist Review (1987) *Sexuality: A Reader.* London. Virago.

Fernando, P. (1988) *Race and Culture in Psychiatry.* London: Routledge and Kegan Paul.

Festau, M. (1975) *The Male Machine.* New York: Delta Books.

Finch, J. (1982) A Women's Health Group in Mansfield in *Women in Collective Action*, edited by Curno *et al.* London: Routledge & Kegan Paul.

Finch, J. (1983) Can Skills Be Shared? Pre-School Playgroups in Disadvantaged Areas in *The Community Development Journal* 18(3), pp. 251–256.

Finch, J. (1984) Community Care: Developing Non-Sexist Alternatives, in *Critical Social Policy*, Issue 9, Spring, pp. 6–18.

Finch, J., and Groves, D. (eds.) (1983) *A Labour of Love: Women Work and Caring.* London: Routledge & Kegan Paul.

Finch, S. (1986) Socialist Feminism and Greenham in *Feminist Review*, No. 23, June, pp. 93–100.

Finn, D. (1985) *The Community Programme.* London: Centre for the Unemployed.

Fisher, R. and Kling, J. M. (198) Leading the People: Two Approaches to the Role of Ideology in Community Organising in *Radical America*, Vol. 21, No.1., pp. 31–45.

Foster, P. (1989) Improving the Doctor-Patient Relationship: A Feminist Perspective in *The Journal of Social Policy.* Vol. 18, Part 3, July, pp. 337–362.

Foucault, M. (1978) *The History of Sexuality.* London: Allen and

Unwin.

Francis, D., Henderson, P. and Thomas, D. (1985) A Survey of Community Workers in the United Kingdom: Some Reflections in *The Community Developmental Journal*, 20(4), pp. 267–273.

Frankfort, I. (1972) *Vaginal Politics*. New York: Quadrangle Books.

Freud, S. (1977) *On Sexuality*. Pelican Freud Library, Vol. 7. London: Penguin.

Frazer, H., Remfrey, P., and Williams, G. (1979) Looking Back – A Personal View from Three Practitioners in *The Community Development Journal*, 14(3), pp. 181–191.

Friedan, B. (1963) *The Feminine Mystique*. New York: Dell.

Fryer, P. (1984) *Staying Power: The History of Black People in Britain*. London: Pluto Press.

Gallagher, A. (1977) Women and Community Work, in *Women in the Community*, edited by Mayo. London: Routledge & Kegan Paul, pp. 121–141.

Gannage, C. (1986) *Double Day, Double Bind*. Toronto: Women's Press.

Gavron, H. (1966) *The Captive Wife*. London: Routledge & Kegan Paul.

Gellhorn, M. (1986) *The Face of War*. London: Virago.

Gillian, C. (1982) *In a Different Voice: Psychological Theory and Women's Development*. Cambridge, Mass.: Harvard University Press.

Gilroy, P. (1987) *There Ain't No Black in the Union Jack*. London: Hutchinson.

Ginsburg, N. (1979) *Class, Capital and Social Policy*. London: Macmillan.

Glampson, A., Scott, T., and Thomas, D. (1976) *A Guide to the Assessment of Community Needs and Resources*. London: National Institute of Social Work.

Glazer, N. (1988) *The Limits of Social Policy*. Cambridge, Mass.: Harvard University Press.

Glendinning, C., and Millar, J. (1987) *Women and Poverty in Britain*. Brighton: Wheatsheaf.

Goodman, J. A. (ed.) (1975) *The Dynamics of Racism in Social Work Practice*. Washington, D.C.: NASW Publications.

Gordon, L. (1976) *Women's Body, Women's Right*. New York: Penguin.

Gordon, P., and Klug, F. (1986) New Right, New Racism in *Searchlight*.

Gordon, P., and Newnham, A. (1985) *Passport to Benefits: Racism in Social Security*. London: Child Poverty Action Group and the Runnymede Trust.

Griffiths, J. (1974a) Carrying On in the Middle of Violent Conflict: Some Observations of Experiences in Northern Ireland in *Community Work One* edited by Jones and Mayo. London: Routledge and Kegan Paul.

Greenwood, V. and Young, J. (1976) *Abortion in Demand.* London: Pluto Press.

Griffiths, H. (1974b) The Aims and Objectives of Community Development in *The Community Development Journal*, 9(2), pp. 88–95.

Griffiths, H. (1975) Community Development: Some More Lessons From the Recent Past in Northern Ireland in *The Community Development Journal*, 10(1), pp. 2–13.

Griffiths, H. (1977) *Lessons from Community Development.*

Griffiths, R. (1988) *(Griffiths Report) Community Care: Agenda for Action.* Norwich: HMSO.

Gulbenkian Foundation Community Work Group (1968) *Community Work and Social Change: A Report Training.* London: Longman.

Gulbenkian Foundation Community Work Group (1973) *Current Issues in Community Work.* London: Gulbenkian Foundation/ Routledge & Kegan Paul.

Guru, S. (1987) An Asian Women's Refuge in *Social Work with Black Children and their Families* edited by Ahmed *et al.* London: Batsford.

Hadley, R., Cooper, M., Dale, P. and Stacey, G. (1987) *A Community Social Worker's Handbook.* London: Tavistock.

Hadley, R. and Hatch, S. (1981) *Social Welfare and the Failure of the State: Centralised Social Services and Participation.* London: Allen and Unwin.

Hadley, R. and McGrath, M. (1980) *Going Local: Neighbourhood and Social Services.* London: Bedford Square Press.

Hanmer, J. (1977) Community Action, Women's Aid and the Women's Liberation Movement, in *Women in the Community*, edited by, Mayo. London: Routledge & Kegan Paul. pp. 91–108.

Hanmer, J., Radford, J., and Stanko, E. (1989) *Women, Policing and Male Violence.* London: Routledge.

Hanmer, J. and Saunders, S. (1984) *Well-Founded Fear: A Community Study of Violence to Women.* London: Hutchinson.

Hanmer, J. and Statham, D. (1989) *Women and Social Work: Towards a Woman Centred Practice.* London: Macmillan.

Hall, C. (1974) *How to Run a Pressure Group.* London: Aldine Press.

Hall, S., Critcher, C., Jefferson, R., Clarke, J., and Roberts, B. (1979) *Policing the Crisis.* London: Macmillan.

Handler, J. (1973) *The Coercive Social Worker: British Lessons for American Social Services.* London: Rand McNalley.

Halpern, M. (1963) *The Politics of Social Change in the Middle East and North Africa.* Princeton: University Press.

Haringey Community Relations Committee (1979) *Report on the Ethnic Elderly.* Haringey: CCRC.

Hearn, J. (1987) *The Gender of Oppression.* Brighton: Wheatsheaf.

Heenan, C. (1988) *An Analysis of a Feminist Therapy Centre.* MA Thesis at Warwick University.

Henderson, P., Jones, D., and Thomas, D. N. (1980) *The Boundaries of Change in Community Work*. London: Allen and Unwin.

Henriques, J. (1984) *Changing the Subject*. London: Methuen.

Hicks, C. (1988) *Who Cares: Looking After People at Home*. Routledge.

Higgins, J. (1989) Caring for the Carers in *The Journal of Social Administration*, Summer, pp. 382–398.

Hinton, W. (1966) *Fanshen*. New York: Vintage Books.

Hooks, B. (1984) *Feminist Theory: From Margin to Center*. Boston: South End Press.

Hopkins, J. (1987) Alternative Services Which Aim to Affirm an Ethnic Identity in *Social Work Today*, No. 23.

Hopkins, M. (1982) *Homeworking Campaigns: Dilemmas and Possibilities in Working with a Fragmented Community*, unpublished MA dissertation. Coventry: The University of Warwick.

Horn, J. S. (1969) *Away with all Pests*. New York: Monthly Review Press.

Howe, D. (1986) The Segregation of Women and their Work in the Personal Social Services, in *Critical Social Policy*, Issue 15, Spring, pp. 21–35.

Hunt, M. (1990) The De-eroticization of Women's Liberation: Social Purity Movements and the Revolutionary Feminism of Sheila Jeffreys in *Feminist Review*, No. 34, Spring, pp. 23–46.

Howell, E., and Bayes, M. (eds.) (1981) *Women and Mental Health*. New York: Basic Books.

Iliffe, S. (1985) The Politics of Health Care: The NHS Under Thatcher in *Critical Social Policy*, Issue 14, pp. 57–72.

Inequality of Sacrifice: The Impact of the Reagan Budget on Women. (1984) Washington: Coalition on Women and the Budget.

Irwin, I. (1971) *The Story of the Womens Party*. New York: Harcourt and Brace.

Jacobs, S. (1984) Community Action and the Building of Socialism from Below: A Defense of the Non-directive Approach in *The Community Development Journal*, 19(4), pp. 217–224.

Janssen-Jurreit, M. (1976) *Sexism: The Male Monopoly on History and Thought*. London: Pluto.

Jones, D., and Mayo, M. (eds.) (1975) *Community Work Two*. London: Routledge & Kegan Paul.

Johnson, N. (1989) The Privatisation of Welfare in *The Journal of Social Policy and Administration*, Vol. 23, No. 1, May.

Joyce, P., Corrigan, P., and Hayes, M. (1987) *Striking Out: Trade Unionism in Social Work*. London: Macmillan.

Kay, S. *et al* (1981) *22 Main Street, Newton, Derbyshire*. Derby: Unpublished paper for Derbyshire Social Services.

Kelly, L. (1988) *Surviving Sexual Violence*. Cambridge: Polity Press.

Klein, R. D. and Steinberg, D. L. (1989) *Radical Voices: A Decade of Feminist Resistance from Women's Studies International Forum*. New York: Athene Press.

Kramer, R., and Specht, H. (1969) *Readings in Community Organisation Practice.* New York: Prentice-Hall.

Kuhn, M. (1984) Challenge to a New Age in *Readings in the Political Economy of Aging* edited by Minkler and Carroll. Farmingdale, N.Y.: Baywood.

Kwo, E. M. (1984) Community Education and Community Development in Cameroon: The British Colonial Experience, 1922–1961 in *The Community Development Journal*, 19(4), pp. 204–213.

Land, H. (1976) Women: Supporters or Supported in *Sexual Divisions and Society* edited by Barker and Allen. London: Tavistock.

Leaper, R. A. B. (1971) *Community Work.* London: National Council of Social Service.

Lederer, L. (1982) *Take Back the Night: Women on Pornography.* New York: Bantam Books.

Lawrence, E. (1977) The Working Women's Charter Campaign, in *Women in the Community*, edited by Mayo. London: Routledge & Kegan Paul, pp. 12–24.

Leeds Social Security Cuts Campaign (LSCC) (1986) *The Campaign Against The Fowler Review.* Leeds: LSCC.

Leissner, A. and Joslin, J. (1974) Area Team Community Work: Achievement and Crisis in *Community Work One* edited by Jones and Mayo. London: Routledge and Kegan Paul.

Leonard, P. (1975) *The Sociology of Community Action.* Keele: University of Keele.

Lerner, G. (1972) *Black Women in White America.* New York: Pantheon.

Lewin, E., and Olesen, V. (eds) (1985) *Women, Health and Healing.* London: Tavistock.

Lewycka, M. (1986) The Way They Were in *New Socialist*, 36 March.

Livingstone, K. (1984) Fifth Column, *New Socialist*, 19, p. 6.

Livingstone, K. (1987) *If Voting Changed Anything, They'd Abolish It.* London: Collins.

London-Edinburgh Weekend Return Group (LEWRG) (1979) *In and Against the State.* London: Pluto Press.

London Women's Liberation Campaign (LWLC) (1979) *Demands for Working Women: The Working Women's Charter.* London: LWLC.

Loney, M. (1977) A Political Economy of Citizen Participation, in *The Canadian State: Political Economy and Political Power* edited by Panitch. Toronto: University of Toronto Press.

Loney, M. (1983) *Community Against Government: The British Community Development Project 1968–1978: A Study of Government Incompetence.* London: Heinemann.

Loney, M. (1986) *The Politics of Greed: The New Right and the Welfare State.* London: Pluto Press.

Longress, J., and McLeod, E. (1980) Consciousness-Raising and

Social Work Practice in *Social Casework*, Vol. 61, No. 5, May, pp. 267–277.

Lorde, A. (1984) *Sister Outsider*. New York: The Crossing Press.

Lovett, T. and Percival, R. (1982) Politics, Conflict and Community Action in Northern Ireland in *Political Issues and Community Work* edited by Curno. London: Routledge and Kegan Paul.

Luker, K. (1984) *Abortion and the Politics of Motherhood*. Berkely: University of California Press.

McConville, M. and Baldwin, J. (1982) The Influence of Race on Sentencing in England in *The Criminal Law Review*, pp. 652–658.

McCrindle, J. Women and the Labour Party, *Beyond the Fragments*, Bulletin 3, p. 17.

McCrindle, J., and Rowbotham, S. (1986) More Than Just a Memory, *Feminist Review*, No. 23, Summer, pp. 109–121.

McIntosh, M. (1981) Feminism and Social Policy, in *Critical Social Policy*, Vol. 1, No. 1., Autumn.

McLeod, E. (1982) *Women Working: Prostitution Now*. London: Croom Helm.

McLeod, E. (1987) *Women's Experience of Love: The Significance of Feminist Therapy*. (Research in Progress).

McNeil, S. and Rhodes, D. (eds) (1985) *Women Against Violence Against Women*. London: Only Women Press.

Mair, G. (1986) Ethnic Minorities, Probation and Magistrates' Courts in *The British Journal of Criminology*, Vol. 26.

Mair, G. (1988) Interpreting Probation Practice with Ethnic Minorities and Women in *The Home Office Research Bulletin*, No. 25.

Malek, F. (1985) *Asian Women and Mental Health or Mental Ill Health: The Myth of Mental Illness*. Southwark: Asian Women's Aid.

Mama, M. (1989) Violence Against Black Women. Gender, Race and State Responses in *Feminist Review*, No. 32, Summer, pp. 30–48.

Mann, K. (1986) The Making of a Claiming Class: The Neglect of Agency in Analysis of the Welfare State, in *Critical Social Policy*, Issue 15, Spring, pp. 62–74.

Manning, B., and Ohri, A. (1982) Racism – The Response of Community Work in *Community Work and Racism* edited by Ohri and Manning, London: Routledge and Kegan Paul.

Marchant, H. and Wearing, B. (eds.) (1986) *Gender Reclaimed*. Sydney: Hale and Iremonger.

Marris, P. (1987) *Meaning and Action: Planning and Conceptions of Change*. London: Routledge and Kegan Paul.

Marris, P., and Rein, R. (1974) *Dilemmas of Social Reform*. New York: Penguin.

Marsden, D. and Oakley, P. (1982) Radical Community Development in the Third world in *Community Work and the State* edited by Craig *et al*. London: Routledge and Kegan Paul.

Marx, K. 91965) *Capital*, Vol. 1, Moscow: Progressive Publishers.

Maynard, A. and Bosanquet, N. (1986) *Public Expenditure in the National Health Service: Recent Trends and Future Problems*. London: Institute of Health Services Management.

Mayo, M. and Jones, D. (1974) *Community Work One*. London: Routledge and Kegan Paul.

Mayo, M. (1975) Community Development: A Radical Alternative in *Radical Social Work* edited by Bailey and Brake. London: Edward Arnold, pp. 129–143.

Mayo, M. (ed.) (1977) *Women in the Community*. London: Routledge and Kegan Paul.

Mayo, M. (1982) Community Action Programmes in the Early Eighties, in *Critical Social Policy*, Vol. 1, No. 3, Spring, pp. 25–40.

Mellor, H. (1985) *The Role of Voluntary Organisations in Social Welfare*. London: Croom Helm.

Merram, E. (1971) *Growing up Female in America: Ten Lives*. New York: Doubleday.

Metcalf, A. and Humpheries, M. (1985) *The Sexuality of Men*. London: Pluto.

Miller, A. (1983) *For Your Own Good: Hidden Cruelty in Childbearing and the Roots of Violence*. New York: Faber and Faber.

Miller, A. S. (198) Saul Alinsky: America's Radical Reactionary in *Radical America*, Vol. 21, No. 1, pp. 11–20.

Millett, K. (1969) *Sexual Politics*. London: Abacus/Sphere. (1972).

Minkler, M., and Carroll, L. E. (1984) *The Political Economy of Aging*. Farmingdale, N.Y.: Baywood.

Mishkind, M. E. (1987) The Embodiment of Masculinity in *Changing Men* edited by Kimmel. London: Sage.

Mitchell, J. (1971) *Women's Estate*. London: Penguin.

Mitchell, J. and Oakley, A. (eds.) (1976) *The Rights and Wrongs of Women*. London: Penguin.

Mitchell, J. and Oakley, A. (eds.) (1986) *What is Feminism?* Oxford: Basil Blackwell.

Moreno, K., Pedrosa, C., Stiles, J. and Lamming, A. (1982) Resident Domestic Campaign in *Women in Collective Action* edited by Curno *et al.* London: Association of Community Workers, pp. 80–88.

Morgan, R. (1971) *Sisterhood is Powerful*. New York: Vintage Books.

Morgan, R. (1984) *Sisterhood is Global*. New York: Anchor Books.

Morgan, P. (1981) From Battered Wife to Program Client: The State's Shaping of Social Problems in *Kapitalistate*, Vol. 9, pp. 17–39.

Moss, P. (1988/9) The Indirect Costs of Parenthood: A Neglected Issue in Social Policy, in *Critical Social Policy*, Issue, pp. 20–37.

Mullard, C. (1973) *Black Britain*. London: George Allen and Unwin.

Muller, J. (1987) The Soup Kitchen: A Critique of Self-Help, in *The Community Development Journal*, No. 22, pp. 36–45.

National Childcare Campaign (NCC) (1984) *National Childcare Campaign Annual Report*. London: NCC.

National Childcare Campaign (NCC) (1985) *National Childcare Campaign Policy Statement*. London: NCC.

National Women's Health Network (NWHN) (1983) The Depo-Provera Debate in *Network News*, March–April, No. 8, pp. 8–10.

Nelson, S. (1982) *Incest, Fact and Myth*. Edinburgh: Stramullion Press.

Nett, E. (1982) *Women as Elders*. Toronto: Resources for Feminist Research.

New York Times (1984) The Colour Line in Old-Age Care, (1984), January 29.

Ng, R. (1988) *The Politics of Community Services: Immigrant Women, Class and State*. Toronto: Garamond Press.

Ng, R., Walker, G., and Muller, J. (eds.) (1989) *Community Organisation and the Canadian Welfare State*. Toronto: Garamond Press.

North Yorkshire Women Against Pit Closures, *Strike 84–85*. Leeds: North Yorkshire Women Against Pit Closures.

Norman, A. (1985) *Triple Jeopardy: Growing Old in a Second Homeland*. London: Centre for Policy on Ageing.

Norton, A., Stotten, B., and Taylor, H. (1986) *Councils of Care: Planning a Local Government Strategy for Older People*. London: Centre for Policy on Ageing.

O'Malley, J. (1977) The Housing Struggle of Two Women, in *Women in the Community*, edited by Mayo. London: Routledge and Kegan Paul, pp. 52–60.

O'Malley, J. (1977) *The Politics of Community Action*. Nottingham: Spokesman Books.

Oakley, A. (1972) *Sex, Gender and Society*. London: Temple Smith.

Oakley, A. (1974) *The Sociology of Housework*. London: Martin Robertson.

Ohri, A., and Manning, B. (1982) *Community Work and Racism*. London: Routledge & Kegan Paul.

Older Women's League (OWL) (1986) *Family Caregivers – A Fact Sheet*. November.

Panitch, L. (ed.) (1977) *The Canadian State: Political Economy and Political Power*. Toronto: University of Toronto Press.

Papadakis, E., and Taylor-Gooby, P. (1988) *The Private Provision of Public Welfare*. Brighton: Wheatsheaf.

Parmar, P. (1986) Can Black and White Women Work Together, in *Spare Rib*, No. 168, July p. 20.

Parry, N., Rustin, M., Satymurti, C. (1979) *Social Work, Welfare, and the State*. London: Edward Arnold.

Parton, C., and Parton, N. (1988/9) Women, the Family and Child Protection in *Critical Social Policy*, Issue, 24, Winter, pp.

38–49.

Peek, E. (1971) *The Baby Trap*. New York: Pinnacle Books.

The People's Plan for the Royal Docks (1983). London: Newham Docklands Forum and GLC Popular Planning Unit.

Perrigo, S. (1986) Socialist Feminism and the Labour Party: Some Experiences from Leeds in *Feminist Review*, No. 23, June, pp. 93–100.

Petchey, R. (1986) The Griffiths Reorganisation of the National Health Service: Fowerlism by Stealth? in *Critical Social Policy*, Issue 17, Autumn, pp. 87–101.

Phillipson, C. (1982) *Capitalism and the Construction of Old Age*. London: Macmillan.

Physician Task Force on Hunger in America (1985) *Hunger in America: The Growing Epidemic*. Boston: Harvard University School of Public Health.

Piven, F., and Cloward, R. (1971) *Regulating the Poor: The Functions of Public Welfare*. New York: Vintage Books.

Piven, F. and Cloward, R. (1977) *Poor People's Movement: Why they Succeed, How They Fail*. New York: Vintage Books.

Planning for the Inner City. (1976) London: HMSO.

Plant, R. (1974) *Community and Ideology: An Essay in Applied Philosophy*. London: Routledge and Kegan Paul.

Plummer, J. (1978) *Divide and Deprive*. London: Joint Council for the Welfare of Immigrants.

Porter, J. (1965) *The Vertical Mosaic: An Analysis of Social Class and Power in Canada*. Toronto: University of Toronto Press.

Power, C., and File, N. (1981) *Black Settlement in Britain: 1555–1958*. London: Heinemann.

Rack, P. (1982) *Race, Culture and Mental Disorder*. London: Routledge and Kegan Paul.

Remfrey, P. (1979) North Tyneside Community Development Project in *The Journal of Community Development*, 14(3), pp. 186–189.

Rex, J., and Moore, R. (1967) *Race, Community and Conflict: A Study of Sparkbrook*. Oxford: Oxford University Press.

Riley, D. (1983) The Serious Burden of Love? Some Questions on Child-Care Feminism and Socialism, in *What is to be Done about the Family?* edited by Segal. London: Penguin.

Roberts, H. (1982) *Doing Feminist Research*. Routledge.

Rooney, B. (1987) *Resistance or Change?* Liverpool: Liverpool University.

Rose, H. (1973) Up Against the Welfare State: Claimants Unions in *The Socialist Register*, pp. 179–207.

Rosenthal, H. (1983) Neighbourhood Health Projects: Some New Approaches to Health and Community Work in Parts of the United Kingdom in *The Community Development Journal*, 18(4), pp. 120–131.

Rosser, S. (1988) *Women, Health and Reproduction*. London: Routledge and Kegan Paul.

Rothman, J. (1970) Three Models of Community Organisation Practice in *Strategies of Community Organisation* edited by Cox *et al*, Itaska, Il.: Peacock Publishing, pp. 20–36.

Rowbotham, S. (1973) *Woman's Consciousness, Man's World*. London: Penguin.

Rowbotham, S. (1979) The Women's Movement and Organising for Socialism, in *Beyond the Fragments* edited by Rowbotham *et al*. London: Newcastle Socialist Centre and Islington Community Press, pp. 9–87.

Rowbotham, S., Segal, L. and Wainwright, H. (1980) *Beyond the Fragments: Feminism and the Making of Socialism*. London: Merlin.

Ruzek, S. (1978) *The Women's Health Movement*. New York: Praeger.

Ruzek, S. (1986) Feminist Visions of Health: An International Perspective in *What is Feminism?* edited by Mitchell and Oakley. Oxford: Basil Blackwell.

Savage, W. and Leighton, J. (1986) *Savage Enquiry*. London: Virago.

Schreader, A. (1984) The Women's Movement and the State: The Political Terrain of Struggle, Unpublished Research Paper, School of Social Work, Carleton University.

Schur, E. M. (1983) *Labelling Women Deviant: Gender, Stigma, and Social Control*. Philadelphia: Temple University Press.

Scottish Women's Aid Federation (SWAF) (1980) *Report from Battered Women and the State Conference*. Edinburgh: December.

Scull, A. (1977) *Decarceration: Community Treatment and the Deviant: A Radical View*. Englewood Cliffs, N.J.: Prentice Hall.

Seebohm, Lord (1968) *(The Seebohm Report) Report of the Committee on Local Authority and Allied Personal Social Services. CMND 3703*. London: HMSO.

Segal, L. (1980) A Local Experience, in *Beyond the Fragments* edited by Rowbotham *et al*. London: Merlin.

Segal, L. (1983) Smash the Family? Recalling the Sixties, in *What is to be Done about the Family?* edited by Segal. London: Penguin.

Segal, L. (ed.) (1983) *What is to be Done about the Family?* London: Penguin.

Segal, L. (1987) *Is the Future Female? Troubled Thoughts on Contemporary Feminism*. London: Virago.

Senate Sex Equality Committee (SSEC) (1986) *Sex Equality Committee Report*. Coventry: The University of Warwick Senate Papers.

Senate Sex Equality Committee (SSEC) (1989) *Sex Equality Committee Report*. Coventry: The University of Warwick Senate Papers.

Sherman, J. and Beck, E. (eds.) (1979) *The Prism of Sex: Essays in the Sociology of Knowledge*. Wisconsin: University of Wisconsin Press.

Shooter, J. and Gergen, K. (eds.) (1989) *Texts of Identity*. London:

Sage.

Sichtermann, B. (1986) *Femininity, the Politics of the Personal*. Cambridge: Polity Press.

Sidel, R. (1972) *Women and Child Care in China*. New York: Hill and Wang.

Sidel, R. (1986) *Women and Children First*. New York: Penguin.

Sidel, R., and Sidel, V. (1977) *A Healthy State: An International Perspective on the Crisis in United States Medical Care*. New York: Pantheon Books.

Sidel, R., and Sidel, V. (1982) *The Health of China*. Boston: Beacon Press.

Sivanandan, A. (1976) Race, Class and the State: the Black Experience in Britain in *Race and Class* 17(4), p. 364.

Skeffington, Lord (1969) *(The Skeffington Report) People and Planning*. London: HMSO.

Skinner, D., and Langdon, J. (1975) *The Clay Cross Story*. London: Penguin.

Sklair, L. (1975) The Struggle Against the Housing Finance Act, in *Socialist Register*, pp. 250–292.

Smale, G., Tuson, G., Cooper, M., Warde, M., Crosbie, D. (1988) *Community Social Work: Paradigm for Change*. London: NISW.

Small, J. (1984) The Crisis in Adoption in *International Journal of Psychiatry*, Vol. 30, Spring, pp. 129–41.

Smith, D. E. (1974) The Social Construction of Documentary Reality, *Sociological Inquiry*, No. 44, pp. 257–268.

Smith, D. E. (1975a) What it Might to do a Canadian Sociology: The Everyday World as Problematic, *Canadian Journal of Sociology*, 3, pp. 363–376.

Smith, D. E. (1975b) An Analysis of Ideological Structures and How women are Excluded: Considerations for Academic Women, *Canadian Review of Sociology and Anthropology*, No. 12, pp. 353–369.

Smith, D. E. (1978) A Peculiar Eclipsing: Women's Exclusion from Man's Culture, *Women's Studies International Quarterly*, No. 1, pp. 281–295.

Smith, D. E. (1979) A Sociology for Women, in *The Prism of Sex: Essays in the Sociology of Knowledge* edited by Sherman *et al*. Wisconsin: University of Wisconsin Press.

Smith, D. E. (1983) Women, Class and Family, in *The Socialist Register*, pp. 1–44.

Smith, J. (1978) Hardlines and Soft Options in *Political Issues in Community Work* edited by Curno. London: Routledge & Kegan Paul.

Smith, J. (1979) *Organise*. Leicester: National Youth Bureau.

Smith, P. (1988) Meeting the Housing Needs of Elderly Asian People in *Social Work Today*, 4 February.

Snitow, A. (1985) Holding the Line at Greenham, in *Mother Jones*,

February/March, p. 47.

Sondhi, R. (1982) The Asian Resources Centre in *Ethnicity and Social Work* edited by Cheetham. Oxford: Oxford University Press, pp. 165–174.

South London Community Health Projects (SLCHP) (1982) South London Community Health Projects in *Women in Collective Action* edited by Curno, *et al.* London: Association of Community Workers, pp. 113–129.

South Wales Association of Tenants (SWAT) (1982) Community Alive Hurts, in *Women in Collective Action*, edited by Curno *et al.* London: Association of Community Workers, pp. 13–31.

Spallone, P. and Steinberg, D. L. (1987) *Made to Order: Myth of Reproductive and Genetic Progress.* London: Pergamon Press.

Specht, H. (1975) *Community Development in the United Kingdom.* London: Association of Community Workers.

Stack, C. (1975) *All our Kin: Strategies for Survival in a Black Community.* New York: Harper Colophon.

Stanley, L., and Wise, W. (1983) *Breaking Out: Feminist Consciousness and Feminist Research.* London: Routledge and Kegan Paul.

Svedin, A. and Gorosch Tomlinson, D. (1984) They Said We Didn't Exist: West Indian Elderly People in Brixton in *Social Work Today*, 2 April.

Tanner, L. (1970) *Voices from Women's Liberation.* New York: New America Library.

Taylor, D. (1989) Citizenship and Social Power, in *Critical Social Policy*, Issue 26, Autumn, pp. 19–31.

Thompson, E. P. (1977) Postscript 1976 in *Romantic to Revolutionary* by Morris. London: Merlin.

Tobin, A. (1990) Lesbianism and the Labour Party in *Feminist Review*, No. 34, Spring, pp. 56–66.

Tolson, A. (1977) *The Limits of Masculinity.* London: Tavistock.

Torkington, C. (1981) *Women in Action, Preservers of the Status Quo or a Force for Change?* Unpublished MA/CQSW Thesis. Coventry: Warwick University.

Townsend, P. (1979) *Poverty in the United Kingdom.* London: Penguin.

Trevillian, S. (1988/89) Griffiths and Wagner: Which Future for Community Care? in *Critical Social Policy*, 24, Winter, pp. 65–73.

Trivedi, P. (1985) To Deny our Fullness: Asian Women in the Making of History, in *Feminist Review*, 20, pp. 25–39.

Tyneside Rape Crisis Centre Collective (TRCC) (1982) Tyneside Rape Crisis Centre, in *Women in Collective Action*, edited by Curno *et al.* London: Association of Community Workers, pp. 170–181.

Ungerson, C. (1987) *Policy is Personal: Sex, Gender and Informal Care.* London: Tavistock.

The Vancouver Sun (1989) Child Molester Alleges Three Year Old Child Was Sexually Aggressive. November.

Van Den Burgh, N. and Cooper, L. (eds.) (1988) *Feminist Visions of Social Work*. New York: National Association of Social Workers.

Voakers, R. and Fowler, Q. (1989) Sentencing, Race, and SERs in the *West Yorkshire Probation Service Journal*, March 1989.

Wagner, G. (1988) *(The Wagner Report) Residential Care: A Positive Choice*. London: National Institute for Social Work/HMSO.

Walker, A. (ed.) (1982) *Community Care: The Family, The State and Social Policy*. Oxford: Basil Blackwell.

Walker, L. (1979) *The Battered Women*. New York: Harper & Row.

Wallace, L. (1988) Making the Service Sensitive to Ethnic Needs in *Social Work Today*, 22 September 1988.

Wallsgrove, R. (1983) Greenham Common Women's Peace Camp – So Why Do We Still Feel Ambivalent?, *Trouble and Strife*, No. 1, p. 4.

Wandor, M. (1972) *The Body Politic: Women's Liberation in Britain 1969–1972*, London: Stage One.

Ward, E. (1984) *Father-Daughter Rape*. London: The Women's Press.

Waters, R. (1988) Race and the Criminal Justice Process in *The British Journal of Criminology*, Vol. 28, No. 1, Winter.

Weinstein, J. (1986) Angry Arguments Across the Picket Lines: Left Labour Councils and White Collar Trade Unionism, in *Critical Social Policy*, Issue 17, Autumn, pp. 40–59.

Weir, A., and Wilson, E. (1984) The British Women's Movement, *New Left Review*, No. 148, December.

Wells, O. (1979) *Community Work and Caring for Children: A Community Project in an Inner City Local Authority*. Ilkley: Owen Wells.

Whitehouse, P. (1983) Race Bias and Social Enquiry Reports in *The Probation Journal*, Vol. 30, pp. 43–49.

Whitlock, M. J. (1987) 'Five more years of Desolation' in *Spare Rib*. No. 180, July, p. 15.

Whittington, B. (1986) *Sexual Harassment: A Human Rights Issue*. Unpublished Paper. Victoria: The University of Victoria.

Williams, G. (1979) Looking Back on British Community Work Practice in *The Community Development Journal*, 9(3), pp. 189–191.

Williams, R. (1961) *Culture and Society*. London: Pelican.

Willmott, P. and Young, M. (1960) *Family and Class in a London Suburb*. London: Routledge and Kegan Paul.

Wilson, A. (1978) *Finding a Voice*. London: Virago.

Wilson, E. (1977a) *Women and the Welfare State*. London: Tavistock.

Wilson, E. (1977b) Women in the Community, in *Women in the Community*, edited by Mayo. London: Routledge & Kegan Paul, pp. 1–11.

Wilson, E. (1980) Beyond the Ghetto: Thoughts on Beyond the Fragments – Feminism and the Making of Socialism, *Feminist Review*, no. 4, p. 38.

Wilson, E. (1982) Women and Community Care in *Community Care* edited by Walker. Oxford: Basil Blackwell.

Wilson, E. (1983) *What is to be Done about Violence Against Women?* London: Penguin.

Wilson, E. with Weir, A. (1986) *Hidden Agendas: Theory, Politics and Experience in the Women's Movement.* London: Tavistock.

Winwood, M. (1977) Social Change and Community Work: Where Now? in *The Community Development Journal*, 12(1), pp. 4–14.

Winship, J. (1985) A Girl Needs to Get Streetwise: Magazines for the 1980's, *Feminist Review*, No. 21, p. 21–33.

Withorn, A. (198) The Politics of Organising in *Radical America*, Vol. 21, No. 1, pp. 8–10.

Withorn, A. (198) Socialist Analysis and Organising: An Interview with Richard A. Cloward and Frances Fox Piven in *Radical America*, Vol. 21, No. 2, pp. 21–29.

Wolfe, T. (1969) *Mau-Mauing the Flak Catcher.* Berkley: University Press.

Women Oppose the Nuclear Threat (WONT) Something in Common, in (ed.) (1986) Cambridge Women's Peace Collective, *My Country is the Whole World.* London: Pandora.

Worcester, N. and Whatley, M. (1988) The Selling of Women's Health Centres: The Response of the Women's Health Movement in *Women, Health and Reproduction* edited by Rosser. London: Routledge and Kegan Paul.

Worthington, R. (1988) Improving SER Practice: A Systematic Approach to Racism in *The Probation Journal*, December.

Index

empower women 119
England 49, 73
entrepreneurs 25, 26
Equal Economic Opportunities Act 87
equal opportunities 93
equality 50, 75, 95, 123
Ernst, S. 70
European Nuclear Disarmament 112, 116
expert 11, 23, 28

facilities 4, 56–58
familial ideology 114, 120
familial relationships 126
Families for Peace 113
family 3, 43, 87, 97, 126
family life 3, 43
family planning clinics 43, 103
  surveillance of family planning clinics 43
family size 19
federations 4
  city wide federations 4
  national federations 4
feminism 107–109
feminist 2, 38, 45, 49, 89, 108, 109
feminist action on the individual level 68–85
feminist action in the workplace 86–105
feminist activity 5, 40, 47, 79
feminist analysis 71
feminist approaches 68–85
feminist campaigns and networks 5, 36–67
feminist challenge 5, 15, 80
feminist collective organisation 39
feminist community action 2, 12–13, 39, 75,
  124–127
feminist community initiatives 5
feminist community newspaper 55
feminist community work 16
feminist community workers 4, 5, 16, 33, 43, 94
feminist consciousness-raising groups 15
feminist councillors 108, 109–112
feminist critique 81
feminist demands 93
feminist egalitarian principles 111
feminist groups 48, 79, 80
feminist insights 8
feminist initiatives 24, 88
feminist intervention 5, 80, 106
feminist health movement 75–82
feminist networks 33, 108
feminist organisational repertoire 42
feminist organisations 48
feminist peace movement 73, 112–121
feminist perspective 2, 3, 40
feminist political action 106–121
feminist political organisations 109–112
feminist political parties 106–121
feminist political presence 123
feminist prefigurative forms 101–105
feminist principles and techniques 5, 79, 96, 103,
  124
feminist self-help provisions 104
feminist services 33
feminist social action 3, 87, 106
feminist stance 112
feminist strategies 111
feminist theory and action 45
feminist theory and practice 41, 101, 102, 105,
  120, 124
feminist therapist 69, 122
feminist therapy 70–74
feminists 3, 41
Festau, M. 42
fieldworkers 30, 33
Fightback Campaign 81
Finch, J. 9, 48, 78

Finn, D. 25
formal community care 9
Foster, P. 78, 103, 104
Fourth International Congress on Women 49
Frankfort, E. 38
Free Enterprise Zone 18, 24
Freidan, B. 42
Freud, S. 70
Freudian psychology 71
funder 11
funding 4, 22, 50, 77, 80, 85, 103, 104

Gallagher, A. 91
gatekeepers 31
Gateshead 23
gender 7, 41, 49, 62, 75
gender consciousness 100
gender equality 5, 124
gender inequality 41, 100
gender neutral language 41
gender oppression 16, 42, 44, 79, 107, 124, 125
gender specific action 122
gendered social relations 40–43
Gilroy, P. 72
Glazer, N. 28
Gordon, L. 40
Gottlieb, N. 32
grassroots activity 105
Great Leap Forward 88
Greater London 23
Greater London Council 107
Greater London Council Women's Unit 107, 108,
  109
Greenham Common Women 112–121
Greenham Common Women's Peace
  Camp 112–121
Greenwood, V. 36
Grey Panthers 88, 97, 98
Griffiths, J. 6, 15, 26
Griffiths, H. 1
Griffiths Report 27
group 4, 45, 47, 50, 51, 57, 78, 83–85, 95
group dynamics 78
group members 84
Groves, D. 9
Grunwick 46, 47, 124
Guild Socialists 2
Gujurati 22
Gulbenkian Reports 7
gynaecological examinations 80

Hackney 90
Hadley, R. 26, 29
Halpern, M. 5
handicap 7
'hard' issues 3, 4
Hatch, S. 29
health 80, 89
health campaigns 80
health care 15, 100, 126
health care corporations 104
health groups 75, 76, 78, 79
health issues 80
health needs 99, 104
health professionals 75
health services 73, 80
Hearn, J. 72
Heenan, C. 70
hegemony 120
Henderson, P. 7
hierarchical differentiation 33
hierarchical institutions 27–29, 33–35
hierarchical relationships 48, 102, 120
hierarchical structures 111
hierarchy 16, 29, 48, 50, 79, 80

153